Your Epilepsy™

Advice from a distinguished expert in seizures and epilepsy

Ilo E. Leppik, MD

*Director of Research,
MINCEP Epilepsy Care,
Minneapolis, Minnesota,
and
Clinical Professor of Neurology
and Pharmacy,
University of Minnesota,
Minneapolis*

Published by Handbooks in Health Care Co.,
Newtown, Pennsylvania, USA

This book has been prepared and is presented as a service to patients with epilepsy and their families. The information provided reflects the knowledge, experience, and personal opinions of Ilo E. Leppik, MD, Director of Research, MINCEP Epilepsy Care, Minneapolis, Minnesota, and Clinical Professor of Neurology and Pharmacy, University of Minnesota, Minneapolis.

Donna L. Miceli assisted in the writing of this book.

This book is not intended to replace or to be used as a substitute for the complete prescribing information prepared by each manufacturer for each drug. Because of possible variations in drug indications, in dosage information, in newly described toxicities, in drug/drug interactions, and in other items of importance, reference to such complete prescribing information is definitely recommended before any of the drugs discussed are used or prescribed.

International Standard Book Number: 1-884065-81-3

Library of Congress Catalog Card Number: 00-00706

Managing Your Epilepsy™. Copyright© 2000 by Handbooks in Health Care Co., a Division of AMM Co., Inc. All rights reserved. Printed in the United States of America. No part of this book may be used or reproduced in any manner whatsoever, including but not limited to electronic or mechanical means such as photocopying, recording, or using any information storage or retrieval system, without written permission, except in the case of brief quotations embodied in critical articles and reviews. For information, write Handbooks in Health Care, 3 Terry Drive, Suite 201, Newtown, Pennsylvania 18940, (215) 860-9600.
Web site address: www.HHCbooks.com

Table of Contents

Introduction 5

Chapter 1
Epilepsy and Seizures 8

Chapter 2
Epileptic Syndromes 17

Chapter 3
Evaluating Seizures 27

Chapter 4
Drug Treatment for Epilepsy 34

Chapter 5
Surgical Treatment for Epilepsy 72

Chapter 6
Other Treatment Options 79

Chapter 7
Women and Epilepsy 87

Chapter 8
Epilepsy and Quality of Life 97

Glossary 110

Index 115

About the Author

Dr. Leppik is past president of the American Epilepsy Society and past chairman of the Professional Advisory Board of the Epilepsy Foundation (of America). He has published many scientific articles and abstracts, as well as a clinical handbook for physicians and nurses, *Contemporary Diagnosis and Management of the Patient With Epilepsy*®.

Ilo E. Leppik, MD

Dr. Leppik's major research interests include the pharmacology of antiepileptic drugs, epilepsy in the elderly, and surgery for epilepsy.

He is listed in all editions of *The Best Doctors in America*® reference book and his biography is included in *Who's Who of the World*.

Introduction

If you or someone close to you has been diagnosed with epilepsy, you're probably experiencing a bewildering mix of emotions. You may be confused by the technical language your doctor is using but embarrassed to admit you don't understand everything you're told; frightened and unsure about the future; or reluctant to share your concerns with friends and family because of the stigma that is still, regrettably, attached to the word *epilepsy*. All of these emotions, although normal and understandable, can leave you feeling very much alone. By choosing to read this handbook, you've taken an important step toward unraveling this confusing mix of emotions and developing an understanding of this difficult condition.

The first thing you need to know is that you are not alone. According to the Epilepsy Foundation (EFA), approximately 2.3 million Americans have been diagnosed with epilepsy. Of that number, some 300,000 are children aged 14 years or younger, and more than 1 million are women. You also need to know that epilepsy is not a single disease. The term epilepsy actually refers to a group of related disorders that all involve recurrent seizures. That's why many doctors commonly use the term *seizure disorder*, although epilepsy is the medically correct term for recurrent seizures.

Epilepsy and seizures are the most common serious neurologic symptoms affecting all ages. Any disease that affects the central nervous system (CNS) is capable of producing epilepsy, and yet in the list of causes, the

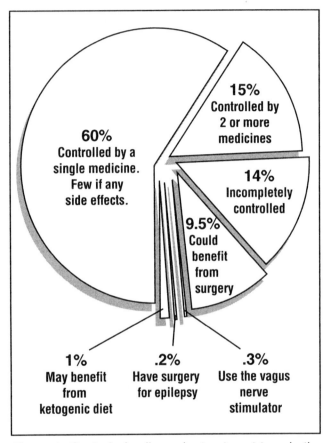

Figure 1: Control of epilepsy by treatment type in the United States (estimated).

most common category is 'unknown.' The most common known causes in the young are genetic syndromes and birth trauma. Cerebrovascular diseases are the most common causes in the elderly. Epilepsy also varies in its degree of severity. Some people have mild epilepsy with seizures that are completely controlled with medicine; others continue to have a few seizures even while taking medication; and still others have uncontrollable epilepsy with multiple seizures despite appropriate treatment (Figure 1).

Most people with epilepsy are completely normal between seizures, but the unpredictability of epileptic episodes, which can cause loss of consciousness and motor control, makes it a frightening condition. Adding to the emotional distress is the fact that epilepsy is misunderstood by many, including some health care professionals. Because of this lack of understanding, patients with epilepsy often face discrimination in the workplace and in society. An experienced doctor will be sensitive to the social and emotional issues you are facing, and will deal with these factors during treatment.

This handbook is not intended to replace the advice of your physician. It is designed to help you become familiar with the medical vocabulary associated with epilepsy and to provide basic knowledge about the various types of seizures, diagnostic techniques, and available treatments. Armed with this knowledge, you can work more effectively with your doctor to find a treatment that will help you live your life as normally and actively as possible. Learning the facts about epilepsy will also help you debunk the myths and erase the stigma associated with this condition.

Chapter 1

Epilepsy and Seizures

Epilepsy, by definition, is a condition in which a person is susceptible to recurrent seizures because of a central nervous system disorder. The key word here is *recurrent*. Seizures are really quite common, affecting about 11% of the population at some point during their lifetime. In fact, anyone can have a single seizure, or convulsion, under certain conditions, including: inadequate blood flow to the brain caused by illness, heart disease, or holding one's breath; high fever, especially in infants and young children; head trauma; or withdrawal from drugs or alcohol. Most people who experience a single seizure do not have epilepsy.

In the normal brain, each neuron, or nerve cell, generates small bursts of electrical impulses that move from neuron to neuron, communicating with the body's muscles, sensory organs, and glands to control all human behavior. In epilepsy, this pattern of neuron activity is disturbed. Instead of firing small bursts of electrical impulses in an ever-changing pattern, a group of nerve cells fires a storm of strong bursts of electricity in rapid succession, like the grand finale of a fireworks display. Normal nerve cells produce electrical impulses up to 80 times a second. In contrast, an epileptic nerve cell can fire up to 500 times a second.

These abnormal discharges can result in a sudden, involuntary change in any activity coordinated by the brain. These changes can include mental confusion, loss of consciousness, and violent, uncontrollable movements of the arms and legs. The clinical signs of a seizure are similar, whether it occurs in a person with epilepsy or is provoked by external circumstances, such as a high fever or head trauma. For this reason, a person having a seizure should be carefully evaluated so that an accurate diagnosis of its cause is established and proper treatment is provided.

Seizures

Over the years, many different terms have been used to describe epilepsy and seizures, including 'fit,' 'spell,' and 'attack.' This has led to unnecessary confusion among patients and doctors. In this handbook, a *seizure* is defined as an abnormal electrical discharge in the brain that can result in a sudden, involuntary change in any activity coordinated by the brain. Remember that most seizures are not epileptic; in other words, they are not associated with a brain disorder. Some seizures that are not epileptic are *physiologic*. This means they occur in response to a physical stress that affects the normal functioning of the body, such as lack of oxygen, lack of sleep, or fever. Other nonepileptic seizures are *psychogenic*, which means they are a reaction to a mental stress, such as physical abuse or sexual abuse, and do not have abnormal electrical discharges in the brain.

There are 2 major categories of epileptic seizures, ie, seizures associated with a brain disorder: partial seizures and generalized seizures. *Partial epileptic seizures* are caused by abnormal activity that is confined to only part of

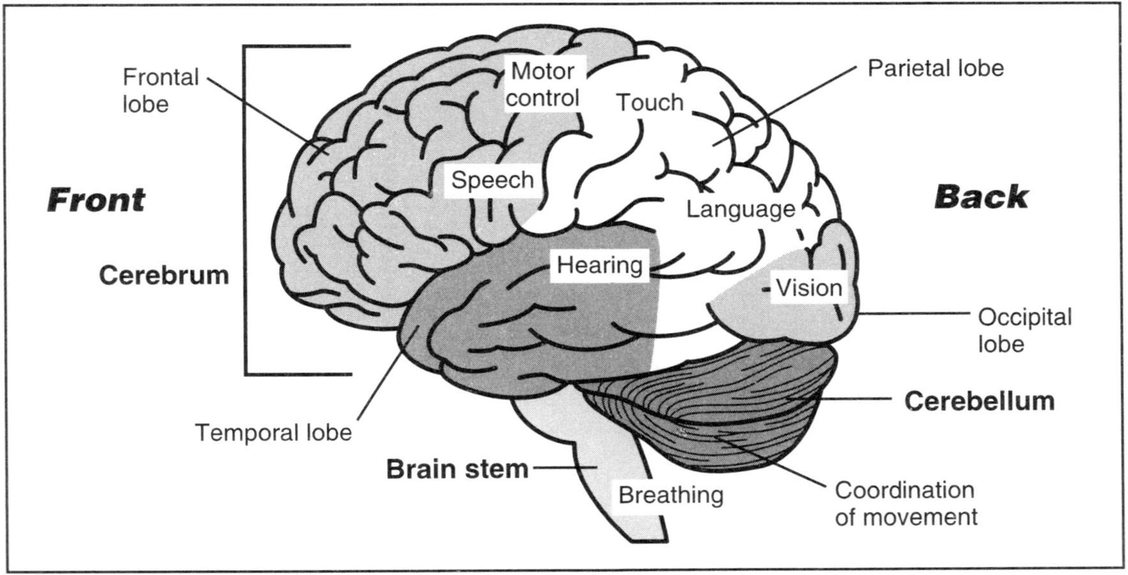

Figure 1: Functional divisions of the brain, as depicted from the left hemisphere.

the brain. The area of the brain involved in a partial seizure is called the *epileptic focus*. In contrast, *generalized epileptic seizures* affect the entire brain at the onset. In many cases, an untreated partial seizure can spread through the entire brain and become a generalized seizure.

Much of the basis for these 2 major categories of epileptic seizures is the recognition that the brain is highly organized, and that specific functions are controlled by separate anatomic regions (Figure 1). Therefore, seizures that originate in a definite region of the brain are classified as partial seizures, and seizures in which no local origin is identifiable are classified as generalized.

These 2 categories of epileptic seizures have been further divided into subtypes that provide the more precise descriptive terms that neurologists use. Your doctor may have used some of these terms when discussing your diagnosis. The most universally accepted classification system for epileptic seizures was developed by the International League Against Epilepsy (ILAE), a worldwide organization of physicians involved in treating epilepsy (Table 1).

Partial Seizures

Partial seizures are subdivided into 3 major categories: simple partial, complex partial, and partial seizures evolving into secondarily generalized seizures. *Simple partial seizures* can be further classified based on their symptoms and their effect on consciousness. Depending on the section of the brain affected, a person experiencing a simple partial seizure may exhibit simple repetitive motions (motor signs), such as hand jerking, and twitching of facial muscles; sensory symptoms such as detecting a strange taste or smell, feeling a breeze, seeing flashing lights, and hearing a buzzing sound; involuntary (autonomic) symptoms, such as nausea, and sweating; or emo-

Table 1: Epileptic Seizures: Classification and Characteristics

I. Partial Seizures (Focal Seizures)
   A. Simple partial seizures
      1. with motor signs
      2. with somatosensory or special sensory symptoms
      3. with autonomic symptoms
      4. with psychic symptoms

   B. Complex partial seizures
      1. simple partial onset followed by impairment of consciousness
      2. with impairment of consciousness at the onset

   C. Partial seizures evolving to secondarily generalized seizures
      1. simple partial seizures
         (a) evolving to generalized seizures
      2. complex partial seizures
         (b) evolving to generalized seizures
      3. simple partial seizures evolving to complex partial seizures evolving to generalized seizures

---

tional (psychic) symptoms such as intense fear, anger, and visual distortions.

Because of the unusual symptoms associated with simple partial seizures, they may be mistakenly identified as signs of a psychological condition. The 3 key features of epileptic seizures that distinguish them from the symptoms of psychiatric disorders are that seizures are short in duration (often only a few seconds or minutes), they occur without warning and without any apparent cause, and they occur in patients who are relatively free of significant psychiatric disorders.

II. Generalized Seizures (Convulsive or Nonconvulsive)
   A. 1. Typical absence seizures (petit mal)
      2. Atypical
   B. Myoclonic seizures
   C. Clonic seizures
   D. Tonic seizures
   E. Tonic-clonic seizures (grand mal)
   F. Atonic seizures

III. Unclassified Epileptic Seizures

- Includes all those seizures that cannot be classified because of incomplete data or because they defy classification into the above categories; for example, neonatal seizures with swimming movements.

IV. Status Epilepticus

- Constant series of seizures.

Used with permission, *Epilepsia 1981;22:489-501.*

Complex partial seizures involve impairment of consciousness (awareness). They may begin as simple partial seizures followed by a change in consciousness, or they may begin with impairment of consciousness, followed by one or more of the signs associated with a simple partial seizure—repetitive motion, involuntary movement, or sensory or emotional symptoms. It's important to understand that loss of, or change in, consciousness with epilepsy is not the same as fainting or being in a coma. Instead, it implies lack of memory or awareness of the event.

An individual may move around in an apparently normal way, but have no awareness of doing so. Sometimes, complicated behaviors occur during a complex partial seizure. These often involve partial undressing, urination, or other socially embarrassing behavior that the patient does not remember after the seizure. Complex partial seizures are often preceded by an eerie sense that something is about to happen, which may be the only thing a patient remembers after the seizure ends.

Most complex partial seizures last for 1 to 3 minutes, but some may last for only a few seconds. These brief epileptic episodes may be confused with a type of generalized seizure, called absence or petit mal, which is discussed in the next section. It's important for physicians to make a clear distinction between the two, because medications used for absence seizures are not effective for complex partial seizures and the medicines for complex partial seizures may worsen partial seizures.

Any partial seizure can evolve to a *secondarily generalized seizure*. In fact, patients rarely seek medical attention for partial seizures. More often, they are brought to the hospital emergency department after an unrecognized and untreated partial seizure progresses to a generalized seizure.

Generalized Seizures

Generalized seizures (affecting the entire brain from the start) can be either convulsive or nonconvulsive. The International Classification of Epileptic Seizures (ICES) recognizes 6 types of generalized seizures: absence (petit mal), which can be typical or atypical; myoclonic; clonic; tonic; tonic-clonic; and atonic.

Absence seizures, which are also called *petit mal seizures*, are most common in childhood. They almost always begin between the ages of 6 and 12, and rarely start after age 20. Absence seizures involve a brief lapse of consciousness, eye-blinking, staring, and other minor facial movements.

Atypical absence seizures involve more noticeable muscle movement, such as rhythmic convulsions, rigidity, or falling down. They may be followed by a period of confusion, and recovery may take longer than with typical absence seizures. Full recovery takes only a few seconds, and there is usually no confusion afterward. The patient also has no memory of the incident.

Because absence seizures usually occur when a child is sitting quietly, he or she may begin to have learning problems before a parent or teacher discovers the seizures. Absence seizures last from a few seconds to a minute, but they may occur many times a day in rapid succession, which can result in poor school performance.

Myoclonic seizures involve quick muscle jerks. They can occur in just one area of the body or in several areas, either simultaneously or one after another. Consciousness is not usually impaired. Although myoclonic seizures can occur alone, they usually occur in specific epilepsy syndromes. Because myoclonic activity may also be associated with other neurologic disorders (eg, lack of oxygen), it can be difficult to categorize.

Tonic seizures involve continuous tightening of the muscles in the face and body, with bending of the arms and extension of the legs. Consciousness is impaired. Tonic seizures are most common in children, and may result in falls.

Clonic seizures are also most common in children. They involve alternate contraction and relaxation of the muscles in rapid succession. Clonic seizures may resemble myoclonic seizures, except that there is a loss of consciousness and the repetition rate of the muscle jerks is slower.

Tonic-clonic seizures, formerly called *grand mal seizures*, are the most dramatic of all seizures. They are the type of seizure most people picture when they hear the word epilepsy. Generalized tonic-clonic seizures begin suddenly and without warning. Typically, a person experiencing a tonic-clonic seizure cries out as the tightening of the muscles in the chest forces air out of the lungs. The tonic phase is characterized by continuous contraction of the muscles, which causes the arms to bend and legs to extend. The tonic phase may last for 15 to 45 seconds, after which short periods of relaxation occur. As the periods of relaxation become more frequent, the clonic phase begins. The clonic phase involves alternate contraction and relaxation of the muscles, often described as *jerking*. The seizure ends with complete relaxation of all muscles in the body. Some, but not all, tonic-clonic seizures are followed by loss of urine as the muscles of the bladder relax. Full consciousness might not return for 10 to 15 minutes, and confusion and fatigue may persist for hours or days.

Atonic seizures are characterized by a sudden loss of muscle tone in the back and legs that causes the person to suddenly drop to the floor. The attacks generally last only a few seconds and can occur without loss of consciousness. These seizures can be dangerous because they have a high rate of injury from falls. It is often difficult to tell the difference between atonic and tonic seizures. Atonic seizures are most commonly seen in children with *Lennox-Gastaut syndrome*, which is an atypical form of absence epilepsy. Epileptic syndromes are explained in the next chapter.

Chapter 2

Epileptic Syndromes

Identifying and classifying epileptic seizures is a complicated process, but it is the most critical step in determining the most appropriate and effective treatment. In an effort to simplify the process, the International League Against Epilepsy (ILAE) revised their original classification system (Table 1, Chapter 1) to include epilepsy syndromes. A *syndrome* is a group of signs and symptoms that collectively characterize an abnormal condition. Correctly diagnosing epilepsy syndromes allows your physician to develop the most effective treatment plan. This is important because a medication that is effective for 1 epilepsy syndrome may have no effect on or even worsen another type.

Epilepsy syndromes are characterized by both the clinical findings and the results of diagnostic testing, which includes the *electroencephalogram* (EEG), and structural and functional studies such as MRI, CAT, PET, and SPECT scans. The clinical findings include:
- Seizure type, or types
- Age when seizure first occurred
- Neurologic findings
- Family history

The EEG is a recording of electrical activity in the brain and provides information on brain wave activity during seizures (the *ictal* phase) and in between seizures (the *interictal* phase). Determining the type of seizure a person is experiencing is the first step in identifying the epilepsy syndrome. Properly classifying a seizure helps your doctor localize the brain regions that are involved, but it is not necessarily useful in determining the underlying cause. Interestingly, more than 1 type of seizure can belong to the same syndrome, and the same type of seizure can occur in different syndromes.

The expanded International Classification of Epilepsies and Syndromes includes 4 categories: localization-related epilepsies and syndromes; generalized epilepsies and syndromes; epilepsies and syndromes undetermined for focal or generalized; and special syndromes. Each of these main categories has a number of subclassifications. The most common are localization-related and generalized.

Localization-Related Epilepsies and Syndromes

There are 2 primary categories of localization-related epilepsies and syndromes: idiopathic with age-related onset, and symptomatic. *Idiopathic,* or *primary,* epilepsies have no known cause. In other words, there is no evidence of injury to the central nervous system (CNS). This raises the possibility of a genetic basis. Some recent discoveries have linked specific gene defects and gene products with idiopathic epilepsy syndromes. Persons with idiopathic or primary forms of various epilepsies usually have a better likelihood for control of seizures than persons with secondary epilepsies once the correct diagnosis is made. Some of these syndromes are also age-specific, ie, they are most active at certain ages, and seizures stop at other ages.

Presently, only 2 syndromes have been established in the idiopathic category, but more may be identified in the future. They are: benign childhood epilepsy with centrotemporal spikes, which your doctor may refer to as *benign rolandic epilepsy*, and childhood epilepsy with occipital spikes.

Benign childhood epilepsy with centrotemporal spikes may account for as many as 25% of epilepsy cases in school-aged children. *Centrotemporal* refers to the region that includes both the central sulcus and the temporal lobe. This syndrome begins between ages 3 and 13, and almost all children outgrow it by age 15. The seizures usually have a simple partial onset, typically beginning in the face and sometimes generalizing to tonic-clonic seizures. The seizures almost always occur at night.

Childhood epilepsy with occipital spikes is much less common. *Occipital* refers to the back part of the brain, which controls vision. This syndrome is characterized by daytime seizures consisting of visual experiences, followed by complex partial seizures. After the seizure, patients often have a headache.

Symptomatic localization-related epilepsies have many specific identifiable causes (Table 1). They are the most common syndromes in adults. Despite the many different causes, seizure types in this category are limited to partial seizures that often, if untreated, progress to secondarily generalized tonic-clonic seizures. The underlying cause may be found in many areas of the brain or in just one area. One syndrome deserves special mention. Mesial temporal lobe sclerosis (MTS) often originates with a febrile seizure in childhood. The child may then not have any seizures until adolescence or early adulthood. MTS involves only 1 temporal lobe and may be corrected surgically.

Table 1: Some Causes of Symptomatic Localization-Related Epilepsies

Vascular
- stroke
- infantile hemiplegia
- arteriovenous malformations
- Sturge-Weber syndrome
- aneurysms (subarachnoid hemorrhage)
- venous thrombosis
- hypertensive encephalopathy
- blood dyscrasias (sickle cell anemia)

Infectious
- abscess
- meningitis and encephalitis
- toxoplasmosis
- rubella
- Rasmussen's syndrome (presumed viral)
- cysticercosis

Tumors
- meningiomas
- gliomas
- hamartomas
- metastatic tumors

Degenerative
- Alzheimer's
- multiple sclerosis

Congenital
- heterotopias
- cortical dysplasias

Traumatic
- prenatal and perinatal injuries
- head injuries

Cryptogenic
- no cause identified

In many cases, the cause of the epilepsy cannot be found. These epilepsies are classified as *symptomatic cryptogenic,* and are the most common syndrome in this category.

Generalized Epilepsies and Syndromes

The generalized epilepsies are most common in children and the different syndromes have different ages of onset. There are 5 subclassifications of generalized epilepsies:

- Idiopathic
- Idiopathic and/or symptomatic
- Symptomatic
- Nonspecific etiology (cause)
- Specific syndromes

The age of onset categories are: newborns, infants, children, and older children and adolescents (juveniles). Numerous syndromes have been assigned to each category (Table 2).

Idiopathic with age-related onset syndromes include: benign neonatal familial convulsions; childhood absence (pyknolepsy); and juvenile myoclonic epilepsy. *Benign neonatal familial convulsions* is a rare syndrome involving generalized seizures that occur only during the first week of life. There is usually a clear family history, and the seizures disappear spontaneously after a few days. Because there are a number of more serious symptomatic seizures that can occur in newborns, careful evaluation is important.

Childhood absence epilepsy used to be called 'petit mal' epilepsy. However, because the term petit mal has been widely misused, the more accurate term 'childhood absence' has been applied to this condition. Because seizures tend to occur many times in an hour, this condition is also described as *pyknolepsy*, from the Greek word *pyknos*, which means thick or frequent. This syndrome, which has a strong genetic link, consists of typical absence seizures (described in Chapter 1). Although the seizures may be short, their rapid succession often leads to learning difficulties because

Table 2: Pediatric Epilepsy Syndromes by Age of Onset

Newborns
- Benign neonatal convulsions (fifth-day fits)
- Familial benign neonatal convulsions
- Early myoclonic encephalopathy
- Severe idiopathic status epilepticus
- Early infantile epileptic encephalopathy with suppression-burst

Infants
- Febrile convulsions
- West's syndrome: infantile spasms
- Benign myoclonic epilepsy in infants
- Severe myoclonic epilepsy in infants
- Myoclonic epilepsy (myoclonic status) in nonprogressive encephalopathies
- Epileptic seizures caused by inborn errors of metabolism
- Myoclonic-astatic epilepsy of early childhood
- Lennox-Gastaut syndrome

Children
- Childhood absence epilepsy (pyknolepsy)
- Epilepsy with myoclonic absences
- Epilepsy with generalized convulsive seizures
- Benign partial epilepsies
- Benign epilepsy with centrotemporal (rolandic) spikes (BERS)
- Benign psychomotor epilepsy
- Benign epilepsy with occipital spike-waves (BEOSW)

Children (continued)
- Other benign partial epilepsies
- Benign partial epilepsy with extreme somatosensory-evoked potentials
- Landau-Kleffner syndrome
- Epilepsy with continuous spikes and waves during sleep
- Epilepsy with photosensitivity
- Eyelid myoclonia absences
- Self-induced epilepsy

Older Children and Adolescents (Juveniles)
- Juvenile absence epilepsy
- Juvenile myoclonic epilepsy (JME)
- Epilepsy with grand mal on awakening (GMA)
- Benign partial seizures of adolescence
- Kojewnikoff's syndrome
- Progressive myoclonus epilepsies
  - Juvenile Gaucher's
  - Juvenile neuronal ceroid lipofuscinosis (NCL)
  - Lafora's body disease
- Unverricht-Lundborg disease (Finnish or Baltic myoclonus epilepsy)
  - Cherry-red spot myoclonus (neuraminidase deficiency)
  - Dyssynergia cerebellaris myoclonica (Ramsay Hunt syndrome)
  - Mitochondrial encephalopathy

of the time that the child loses from school and other learning activities. About 40% of patients with childhood absence epilepsy recover, but others have generalized tonic-clonic seizures that continue into later life.

The syndrome of *juvenile myoclonic epilepsy* (JME) begins during the teenage years and involves 3 types of seizures: myoclonic, absence, and generalized tonic-clonic. Myoclonic seizures usually occur in the morning and primarily involve the arms and hands. The most common complaint is clumsiness or jitters, which are made worse by stress. These seizures are often mistaken for adolescent behavior. Generalized tonic-clonic seizures also usually develop in the morning. Absence seizures can be difficult to detect. Not all people with JME have all 3 types of seizure, but patient history and EEG results—when properly evaluated—usually provide an accurate diagnosis.

Symptomatic and/or idiopathic epilepsy consists of a mixed set of syndromes with similar clinical signs. Some children with these syndromes have symptoms that point to an identifiable cause, while others have seizures for which no cause can be found. Unlike children with idiopathic age-related epilepsy, who have normal intelligence, children in this group often are mentally retarded. Syndromes in this category include infantile spasms and Lennox-Gastaut syndrome.

Infantile spasms, also known as *West's syndrome*, begin between the ages of 4 and 12 months. This syndrome is defined by a specific seizure type that involves bending at the neck, waist, arms, and legs with the arms either drawn away from or drawn toward the body. These spasms last only a second or two and may occur hundreds of times a day. Infants with this syndrome usually develop normally until the spasms occur. Once the spasms begin, the child's psychomotor development is arrested. The clinical outcome for children with infantile spasms depends on the underlying brain disorder causing the seizures and how the infant responds to medical treatment. Among all patients with infantile spasms, 20% die before 5 years of age. Of those who survive, 75% to 93% are reported to be mentally retarded; up to 50% have epilepsy later in life; and half of these develop Lennox-Gastaut syndrome.

Lennox-Gastaut syndrome represents a combination of seizures that include: axial tonic attacks, tonic-clonic seizures, atypical absence seizures, and atonic seizures ('drop attacks'). The onset of Lennox-Gastaut syndrome is between 1 and 8 years, and it is usually difficult to treat. Patients with this syndrome often also have developmental delay.

Epilepsies and Syndromes, Undetermined as to Focal or Generalized

This category includes a number of pediatric syndromes with clinical signs that are not yet fully understood. This includes a number of cases of myoclonic epilepsy with mental retardation.

Special Syndromes

This category includes conditions in which seizures are related to specific stimuli (eg, a flashing light). These patients probably have some dysfunction in the CNS that causes them to react to the stimulus. Treatment for these special syndromes usually involves avoiding the specific stimulus or treating only at the time of exposure to the stimulus. Also included in this group are patients who have isolated seizures and may simply have a low seizure threshold.

Situation-related seizures is another special syndromes category. Febrile seizures, which occur during high fevers, often above 103° F, are the most common of this type of seizure. They usually occur in children between 3 months and 5 years old who have fever but no evidence of another cause for the seizure. Studies indicate that febrile seizures are relatively harmless and are not associated with an increased risk of mental retardation or of serious neurologic disability. The overall chance of epilepsy after febrile seizures is small, with 3% developing epilepsy by 7 years of age and approximately 7% by 25 years of age. The risk of having additional febrile seizures is related to the child's age at the time of the first seizure. Although it is higher in younger children, the overall risk of recurrence is 34%. Among those patients who have their first febrile seizure before the age of 12 months, the chance of a second seizure is 50%.

Medical experts have different opinions about treating febrile seizures. Many pediatric neurologists do not recommend long-term treatment for simple febrile seizures. This is because phenobarbital, which is the most common treatment, has side effects that can be expected to affect up to 40% of patients. Many believe that these side effects offset any potential benefits of treatment. In addition to treating the fever, some doctors recommend use of rectal diazepam in children with high fever who have had previous convulsions associated with fever.

Chapter 3

Evaluating Seizures

Accurately diagnosing the cause of a seizure is a complicated procedure. Your doctor must first find out if the episode is actually an epileptic seizure. The medical community refers to this as 'differential diagnosis,' and it is the most difficult step in the evaluation process. Most events associated with loss of consciousness and abnormal body movements are not epileptic seizures. Almost as difficult is determining whether the seizure indicates the presence of epilepsy. Most persons who have a single seizure do not have epilepsy. In fact, only one third of people who have a seizure have epilepsy. Although a seizure does not necessarily imply the presence of epilepsy, it may be the initial event that does indicate the presence of epilepsy. Remember, epilepsy is a brain disorder that is characterized by seizures.

Fainting or loss of consciousness, or *syncope*, is the most common symptom confused with seizures (Table 1). Because it is often accompanied by brief clonic activity, syncope can easily be confused with seizure disorder.

Other conditions often mistaken for epilepsy include: nonepileptic seizures, which can occur in response to physical or mental stress; breath-holding spells in children, which were once considered possible seizures but

Table 1: Differential Diagnosis of Syncope

1. Vasovagal attack
   - hyperventilation-induced syncope
2. Cardiac
   - atrioventricular block
   - Adams-Stokes attack
   - sinoatrial block
   - paroxysmal tachycardia
   - reflex cardiac arrhythmia
   - other cardiac causes of decreased cardiac output
3. Hypovolemia
4. Hypotension
5. Cerebrovascular ischemia
6. Micturition syncope
7. Other conditions

have been proven to be associated with behavioral problems; sudden, intense spasms that occur during deep sleep; panic attacks; and many other conditions.

Evaluating a Seizure

To determine if a seizure is epileptic or nonepileptic, your doctor will consider a number of things. First, he or she will develop a history of the seizure. He or she will ask you to describe the seizure pattern in detail, including events that happened days before; a complete description of the seizure; the presence of any warning signs (*prodromal symptoms*), which are referred to as

Table 2: Common Causes of Provoked Seizures

- Extreme sleep deprivation
- Excessive use of stimulants, including natural products
- Withdrawal from sedative drugs or alcohol
- Substance abuse (cocaine, 'speed')
- High fever, especially in children
- Low blood sugar (hypoglycemia)
- Electrolyte imbalance
- Lack of oxygen (hypoxia)
- Other causes

auras; and observations about the period immediately following the seizure (*the postictal period*). If you experienced the seizure, you will probably be unable to accurately describe it, so your doctor will want to talk with someone who was present.

It's particularly important for your doctor to determine if the seizure was provoked or unprovoked. Unprovoked means it was sudden and unexpected, occurring without any disturbance in your normal body rhythms. Provoked seizures have an identifiable cause and do not usually signal the presence of epilepsy. These include extreme sleep deprivation, high fever, or excessive use of stimulants. Table 2 lists some common causes of provoked seizures.

Medical History

Your medical history is another important part of the puzzle. Your doctor will want to know if you have ever experienced *febrile convulsions,* which are caused by high fever in childhood. He or she will ask questions about head injury, stroke or heart disease, cancer, use of over-the-counter drugs, herbal products and caffeinated beverages, substance abuse, and infectious disease. In addition, travel, work stress, sleep deprivation, and other factors in your personal life will be evaluated.

Family history is also an important factor. Your doctor will ask questions about your parents, siblings and other close relatives. Have any of your family members experienced febrile convulsions? Do any of your siblings, your parents, or close relatives have epilepsy? Is there a family history of neurologic disorders?

Physical Examination

A physical examination is essential to making an accurate diagnosis. Your doctor will pay particular attention to any pattern of injuries, your cardiovascular system, and your skin. He or she will carefully examine your head for any signs of new or old injury. Scars can be important clues to head injuries or surgeries that may predispose you to seizures or epilepsy. The appearance of your tongue can also reveal important evidence because tongue biting is a common feature of a tonic-clonic seizure. Your doctor will also evaluate your cardiovascular system for signs of disorders. It's not unusual to find patients treated for epilepsy who have a heart or circulatory condition that results in lack of oxygen to the brain. The presence of birth marks or other soft tumors on your skin can also provide clues that will help your doctor make a diagnosis. Other functions your doctor needs to check include: mental status, sensory loss, motor function, and reflexes. In addition, he or she will request laboratory tests of your blood and urine to check for signs of conditions that can cause seizures.

The Electroencephalogram

The electroencephalogram (EEG) was developed in the early 1900s and has played an important role in increasing our understanding of epilepsy. EEG findings, which are referred to as *tracings*, are an invaluable tool in diagnosing seizure disorder. They provide graphic evidence of abnormal electrical activity in the brain before, during, and after a seizure. In most cases, EEG findings can establish the presence of a seizure disorder and indicate its classification. In some cases, they can even suggest the cause. The EEG is safe, painless, and relatively inexpensive, so there's no reason to be overly concerned about it.

The electroencephalograph consists of 3 parts: electrodes, an amplifier, and a recording machine. To produce tracings of your brain waves, electrodes are pasted on different parts of your scalp. These electrodes detect surges in electrical activity in the part of the brain that is under each electrode. The fluctuations from each electrode are amplified and transferred to voltage-sensitive, ink-filled needles that rest on a continually moving piece of paper and/or to a computer screen. Changes in the electrical activity in the various areas of the brain cause the needles to move up and down to record the pattern of changes on the paper. A normal EEG tracing shows a slightly wavy line with only small variations in the height of the waves. In the presence of seizure disorder, the wavy line rises and falls dramatically in a series of peaks (spikes) and valleys (sharp waves). Figure 1 compares a normal EEG with an EEG that indicates seizure disorder.

Your doctor may have you stay awake most of the night before the EEG so you will be extremely tired. Fatigue can be important to the accuracy of the EEG because better readings are obtained if you fall asleep. Also, the fatigue can

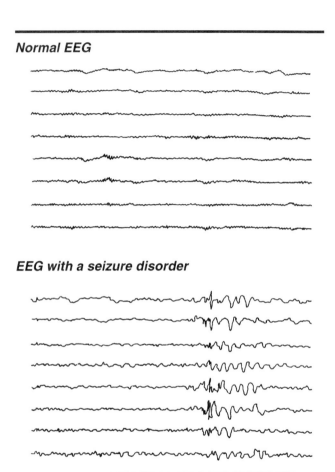

Figure 1: EEG tracings for a normal patient and for a patient with epilepsy.

make abnormalities show up. Strobe lights should be flashed and you should be asked to hyperventilate during the test to see if these stimuli can provoke abnormal brain activity.

Advanced EEG Technology

EEG technology has advanced dramatically over the years. Long-term EEG monitoring can now be conducted on outpatients using specially designed head gear fitted with electrodes. Patients can wear this head gear as they go about their daily activities. Electrical activity in the brain is amplified and converted to electronic signals that are stored on a cassette tape recorder, which patients also wear. An automated data analysis system allows for data to be obtained from the recordings without an observer having to spend hours studying the tapes.

In some cases, a doctor may want to examine the connection between the EEG tracings and the clinical signs of the seizure. This involves using both EEG and video monitoring. Electrodes attached to the patient's head transmit brain-wave activity to recording equipment while a television camera records the patient. The video images and EEG tracings are displayed on a split screen so observers can compare the tracings with the patient's behavior.

CT and MRI Scans

If your doctor suspects that a lesion in your brain caused your seizure, he or she may order either a computed tomography (CT) or a magnetic resonance imaging (MRI) scan. Although both of these radiographic tests provide high-quality pictures of the inside of your head and can depict lesions that may be the cause of seizure disorder, the MRI is much more sensitive.

Chapter 4

Drug Treatment for Epilepsy

Because of recent advances in human and animal research, we have a better chance to control or cure epilepsy than was possible even 10 years ago. Many physicians are not aware of all of these advances, so a patient who continues to experience seizures and has not been evaluated by an epilepsy specialist might benefit from a second opinion.

More new drugs to treat epilepsy have been approved during the past decade than ever before, including felbamate (Felbatol®), gabapentin (Neurontin®), fosphenytoin (Cerebyx®), lamotrigine (Lamictal®), levetiracetam (Keppra™), oxcarbazepine (Trileptal®), tiagabine (Gabitril®), topiramate (Topamax®), and zonisamide (Zonegran™). In addition, new formulations of older drugs, which can be more effective with fewer side effects, have been developed. These include rectal diazepam (Diastat®) and intravenous valproate for use in emergency situations. Sustained-release drugs such as carbamazepine (Tegretol® XR, Carbatrol®) have decreased the swings patients experience between high (peak) and low (trough) levels. Pregabin, a more powerful relative of gabapentin, has completed testing and may be available in 2001. Experimental drugs such as rufinamide and narkosenide are being tested in the United States, and many other drugs are coming close to testing.

In addition, new routes of drug delivery are being explored. These include direct injection of drugs into the cerebrospinal fluid, which bathes the brain. Medication would be administered via an implantable pump loaded with very powerful drugs that could not be taken effectively as pills.

Deciding When to Begin

One of the most difficult decisions a physician faces is when to start treatment for a patient who has experienced a seizure. Your doctor will want to discuss and evaluate a number of issues with you before making that decision. If your seizures are nonepileptic, treatment should be directed at eliminating the underlying cause. If your seizures are epileptic, your doctor must assess the risk of further seizures and balance that against the risks and benefits associated with using antiepileptic drugs (AEDs). Most of the time, AEDs do not cause significant unpleasant side effects. Knowledge of epilepsy syndromes and their usual course will help your doctor make this decision.

In some cases, the decision is obvious. For example, studies have shown that children with certain types of benign epilepsy often outgrow this condition so the risk of medication may not be warranted. On the other hand, medication is an appropriate treatment when a brain tumor or other abnormal growth associated with recurrent seizures is diagnosed. Unfortunately, the decision is rarely that clear-cut, especially when the patient has only suffered one seizure. In these cases, the doctor will con-

sider specific risk factors that can help identify patients who are at higher risk for additional seizures. These risk factors include:
- A sibling with seizures
- An electroencephalogram pattern of generalized spikes and waves
- The occurrence of a previous seizure during an illness
- A history of significant head trauma, stroke, or other central nervous system conditions

If a patient has none of the additional risk factors, the patient and physician must decide whether to treat based on the impact a second seizure would have on the patient's life. For example, treatment may be indicated for patients who need to drive or who face a risk of injury or loss of self-esteem from a second seizure. For adults, one of the most important considerations is driving a motor vehicle. A single seizure usually has not been considered grounds for significant driving restrictions, but the occurrence of 2 or more seizures subjects the patient to numerous restrictions.

After reviewing the odds for recurrence with their physician, some patients choose to begin treatment after a single seizure. There may be less pressure to treat children after a single seizure because driving is not an issue. Identifying a specific epilepsy syndrome in a child can help the physician decide whether to begin treatment.

Choosing an Antiepileptic Drug

About 75% of seizure disorders can be controlled with antiepileptic drugs. There are more than a dozen AEDs on the market, and more are being developed. Some are effective for treating several different types of seizures, and others, especially the newer drugs, are designed to treat specific types of epilepsy. The goal of treatment with

AEDs is to prevent the recurrence of seizures while avoiding side effects from the drugs.

It may take some time for your doctor to find the right drug and dose to control your seizures without causing debilitating side effects. For this reason, it's important that you and your doctor communicate when you set goals and establish a treatment timetable. It's also important that you comply with the treatment schedule. Because there can be long intervals between seizures, with no intervening symptoms, you may be tempted to skip a dose, or even discontinue your medication, without discussing it with your doctor. It's important that you resist that temptation. Noncompliance is the most common cause of treatment failure.

The typical procedure for initiating treatment with an AED is to begin with the lowest recommended dose. If that doesn't control the seizures, your doctor will increase the dose, and/or adjust the dosing schedule. If the highest recommended dose of the selected drug is not effective, or if the side effects are intolerable, your doctor may try the same procedure with a different medication. In some difficult cases, referred to as *intractable* or *refractory*, a combination of 2 or more drugs may be necessary to achieve control. It is usually preferable to just take 1 drug because of the risk of interaction between AEDs and the increase in side effects. However, for some patients, adding a second AED may bring control that one drug can't achieve.

The History of AEDs

Although many potions and herbal products have been used for centuries, the first effective treatment for epileptic seizures was bromide. In 1857, Sir Charles Locock presented evidence of successfully using bromide in female patients

Table 1: Available AEDs

Generic Name	Brand Name(s)
benzodiazepines	Valium®, Lorezapam®
carbamazepine	Tegretol®, Carbatrol®
clonazepam	Klonopin®
diazepam	Valium®
ethosuximide	Zarontin®
felbamate	Felbatol®
fosphenytoin	Cerebyx®
gabapentin	Neurontin®
lamotrigine	Lamictal®
levetiracetam	Keppra™
oxcarbazepine	Trileptal®
phenobarbital	Donnatal®, Quadrinal®, Bellatal®
phenytoin	Dilantin®
primidone	Mysoline®
tiagabine	Gabitril®
topiramate	Topamax®
valproate	Depakote®, Depacon™, Depakene®
zonisamide	Zonegran™

with intractable epilepsy. Others confirmed his experience and soon bromide was being used as primary therapy for epilepsy. Although bromide is effective for controlling seizures, it causes serious side effects, including sedation, depression, skin eruptions, and gastrointestinal distress. Despite this, bromide was the only effective substance known for the treatment of epilepsy for more than 50 years.

Because it is one of bromide's prominent side effects, sedation was once considered essential for anticonvulsant effect. Based on this assumption, phenobarbital, which was developed in 1912, was suggested as a treatment for epilepsy. For the next 25 years, epilepsy was treated with phenobarbital and other drugs associated with slowing of mental function. This may help to explain the incorrect, but once widely held, belief that persons with epilepsy are mentally slow.

In the late 1930s, after researchers discovered the benefits of testing drugs on animals, they learned that sedation and depression are not essential for controlling convulsions. Between 1946 and 1978, 17 drugs for treating epilepsy were approved in the United States. Some were subsequently withdrawn because of toxicity or lack of effectiveness. Most have been found to have only limited usefulness or are infrequently used. Although there were no new major drugs approved for epilepsy between 1978 and 1993, there were important advances in the use of AEDs, including new technology to measure AED concentrations in the blood. This technology has been useful in developing more accurate dosages and in determining patient compliance with the prescribed therapy.

Since 1993, more than 10 new AEDs have been approved for use in the United States and several others are in various stages of approval. Table 1 lists the most widely used AEDs.

What About Side Effects?

Epilepsy can be controlled in most patients without serious side effects. However, it's a fact of life that any medication, even aspirin, has a potential for causing side effects. In most cases, the potential for serious side effects increases as the dose increases. That's why your doctor will begin with the lowest dose of the selected drug that should be effective and, if necessary, increase it gradually until it achieves the desired effect. Very rarely, any medicine can cause an unpredictable very serious side effect which could be fatal.

AEDs have the potential for causing annoying side effects such as dizziness, mild nausea, dry mouth, and drowsiness, which are common with many drugs. However, these effects generally subside in a few days after the body has adjusted to the drug. Be sure to tell your doctor if troublesome side effects continue after a week or two and, especially, if they are seriously affecting your quality of life. He or she can usually prescribe a different medication or can treat the symptoms. *Don't discontinue the medication without first talking with your doctor.*

Safety is a concern when choosing medication. Your doctor would not want to prescribe a medication that could put you in greater jeopardy than the potential harm from continued seizures. Fortunately, the available AEDs are relatively safe when prescribed according to the manufacturers' recommendations.

In addition to the type of seizure, or seizure syndrome, you are experiencing, your doctor will consider a number of factors before selecting an AED. These factors include: your age; your sex (special considerations for female patients is discussed in Chapter 7); other health problems, especially the presence of liver or kidney disease; and other medications you are taking. It's important that you tell your doctor about all medications you are taking, including over-the-counter drugs (OCDs), and herbal and vitamin supplements, to avoid danger.

Once your doctor has decided on an appropriate AED, he or she should provide you with information about the drug. Here are some questions you should

ask before you begin an AED, or any new prescription drug.
- What form of the drug are you prescribing (tablet, capsule, liquid, injectable)?
- How often should I take the drug?
- What are the side effects of this drug?
- What should I do if side effects occur?
- Should I take the drug on an empty stomach or with meals?
- What time of day should I take the drug?
- What should I do if a dose is missed or vomited?
- What other drugs, including OCDs and herbals, are not safe to take with this drug?
- Are there any foods that I should avoid while taking this drug?

After your doctor begins AED treatment, he or she will monitor the level of drug in your blood. This is done to evaluate the effectiveness of the drug and to determine its safety. Your doctor should ask you to record your seizures on a calendar so that he or she can assess the effectiveness of the drug. When you are doing well, with no seizures and no side effects, he or she will check your blood level to establish a guideline, which can be used to determine control. If you continue to do well, your doctor will probably just check your blood annually to make sure there have been no significant changes in the way the drug is affecting your body.

Profiles of Most Common Antiepileptic Drugs

Each AED has specific actions and uses, doses and preparations, side effects, and common drug interactions. A note about dosage: most AED dosages are in milligrams (mg) but other units are sometimes used.

Carbamazepine: Action and Uses

Carbamazepine is effective alone or with other AEDs in partial seizures, especially complex partial seizures, in generalized tonic-clonic seizures, and in combinations of these seizure types. It is ineffective for absence, myoclonic, and atonic seizures. Carbamazepine may worsen some types of generalized seizures.

Clinical data indicate that carbamazepine is better tolerated than phenobarbital and primidone in simple and complex partial seizures, but individual responses vary. This drug is preferred to phenobarbital in pediatric patients because it appears to have less effect than phenobarbital on cognition and behavior.

Peak blood levels of carbamazepine occur in 4 to 12 hours when the drug is taken in solid dosage forms. Significantly larger doses of carbamazepine often are required when it is used in combination with phenobarbital or phenytoin. Extended-release forms such as Tegretol® XR and Carbatrol® are now available in the U.S. These extended-release medications need to be taken only twice daily. Because these forms keep the blood level steady, they may provide better seizure control and fewer side effects.

Dosage and Administration. Oral: Children 6 to 12 years, 100 mg twice daily on the first day. The amount can be increased by 100 mg daily at appropriate intervals (usually 1 to 2 weeks) and given in 3 or 4 divided doses until the desired response is obtained (usual maximum dose, 1,000 mg). The usual daily maintenance dose is 400 to 800 mg (another way to calculate this is 15 to 30 per kilogram or the patient's weight, or mg/kg); the frequency of use must be individualized. For children 4 to 6 years, 10 to 20 mg/kg in 2 or 3 divided doses is warranted, increased by up to 100 mg daily at weekly intervals, as needed and tolerated. The usual maintenance dose is 250 to 350 mg a day (usual maximum dose, 400 mg). For children under 4 years, a starting dose of 20 to 60 mg is recommended.

For adults and adolescents, initially 400 mg should be divided into 2 doses on the first day, increased by 200 mg daily at appropriate intervals (usually 1 to 2 weeks) and administered in 3 or 4 divided doses. The usual daily maintenance dose is 600 mg to 1,200 mg in monotherapy, but may be as high as 2,000 mg in combination therapy.

Although extensive studies are not available, it appears that elderly patients metabolize carbamazepine more slowly and therefore will need lower doses.

Carbamazepine suspension may be given through a nasogastric tube, but this requires careful flushing.

Rectal suspension: can be used for rectal administration.

Generic: tablets 200 mg; chewable tablets 100 mg.

Tegretol® (Novartis): tablets 200 mg; chewable tablets 100 mg; suspension 100 mg/5 mL.

Tegretol® XR: tablets 100, 200, 400 mg.

Carbatrol® 200, 300 mg.

Adverse Reactions and Precautions. Blood and platelet counts, urinalysis, and liver and kidney function studies should be performed before starting treatment with carbamazepine. Blood tests should be done once or twice during the first year of treatment as part of the routine monitoring. Skin reactions such as rashes have been reported in 2% to 4% of patients. Less common but more serious skin reactions may happen and may be fatal.

Less serious side effects that occur during early treatment with carbamazepine are drowsiness, dizziness, lightheadedness, double vision, ataxia (incoordination and unsteadiness), nausea, and vomiting. These usually subside spontaneously within a week or after a reduction in dose.

Less common neurologic reactions include confusion, headache, fatigue, blurred vision, oculomotor disturbances, dysphasia (difficulty in swallowing), abnormal involuntary movements, peripheral neuritis and paresthesias, depression with agitation, talkativeness, nystagmus (involuntary movements of the eyes), and tinnitus (ringing in the ears).

Gastrointestinal reactions include gastric distress and abdominal pain, diarrhea, constipation, and anorexia. Dryness of the mouth, glossitis, and stomatitis also occur.

Temporary low white blood counts occur in about 10% of patients treated with carbamazepine, but stopping the drug usually is not required. Patients should notify their physician if fever, sore throat, easy bruising, purple or red spots on the skin, or other signs of blood toxicity appear.

Carbamazepine has an effect on sodium balance that may be troublesome, particularly in cardiac or elderly patients.

Drug Interactions. Carbamazepine increases the liver's metabolism of clonazepam, diazepam, ethosuximide, and valproate. In patients treated with phenobarbital, phenytoin, or primidone concomitantly, a small increase or, more commonly, a decrease in the blood levels of one or both agents may occur.

Carbamazepine levels are markedly increased by erythromycin and propoxyphene hydrochloride. Cimetidine, danazol, diltiazem, isoniazid, propoxyphene, troleandomycin, and verapamil also increase the levels of carbamazepine, but to a lesser degree. In pediatric patients, large doses of nicotinamide may increase carbamazepine plasma levels. Carbamazepine may decrease the effectiveness of oral contraceptives, certain anti-infectives (doxycycline, mebendazole) haloperidol, and theophylline. Carbamazepine also may reduce the levels and therapeutic response to corticosteroids or thyroid hormones. The combination of carbamazepine and lithium may increase the risk of neurotoxicity.

Phenytoin and Fosphenytoin: Actions and Uses

Phenytoin (Dilantin®) is useful in generalized tonic-clonic, complex partial, and simple partial seizures. Clinical trials indicate that phenytoin is better tolerated than phenobarbital and primidone. It is ineffective in absence, myoclonic, and atonic seizures and is not recommended for the treatment of epileptic syndromes in which absence seizures or myoclonus are present. Intravenous fosphenytoin is an effective treatment for status epilepticus and can be used as the initial drug to manage recurrent seizures.

Time to peak levels in the blood varies and increases with the dose, but normally occurs within 4 to 8 hours for prompt-release capsules, and somewhat later for the extended-release preparations.

Dosage and Administration. Oral: The dosage must be individualized according to the patient's response and to the drug concentrations. Phenytoin can be given in divided doses (but does not need to be dosed more than twice daily). In adults, once-daily administration is usually sufficient to maintain effective blood levels. It also improves compliance. However, once-daily dosage may not be practical in patients who tend to miss doses.

For adults, initially 300 mg daily is recommended in 2 divided doses; the maintenance dose is usually 4 to 6 mg/kg/day. Incremental increases can be made using 30-mg capsules. Dosing for the elderly has not been well established but is usually 3 to 4 mg/kg/day lower than those in adults.

For children, initially 5 mg/kg/day is recommended in 2 divided doses, with the maintenance dose individualized. Maintenance doses may need to be higher, 7 mg/kg/day or more.

Phenytoin suspension may be given through a nasogastric tube, but this must be flushed well and clamped after administration.

Intravenous (IV): Phenytoin is very water insoluble and must be administered slowly. Leakage from the injection site into the underlying tissue can cause necrosis. To avoid these problems, fosphenytoin (Cerebyx®), has been developed. It is rapidly converted to phenytoin with a half-life of 8 to 12 minutes. Thus, within 20 to 30 minutes, almost all of the fosphenytoin has been converted to phenytoin in the body. The advantages of this drug are that it is formulated in a water solution, is well tolerated, and does not cause venous sclerosis. Dilantin® solution is no longer available; it has been replaced by Cerebyx®.

Intramuscular (IM): The phenytoin preparation now in use should not be given intramuscularly because it can cause painful and insoluble crystals at the injection site. However, fosphenytoin is readily absorbed after IM injection. It causes little discomfort. The availability of this IM drug has made it possible to replace oral phenytoin in situations where a patient cannot take drugs by mouth, thus also avoiding IV administration. Also, this preparation may be used when a patient has had some seizures and has a low phenytoin level.

Phenytoin:

Generic: Suspension 125 mg/5 mL (alcohol < 0.6%).

Dilantin® (Parke-Davis): Suspension 125 mg/5 mL (alcohol < 0.6%); tablets (chewable) 50 mg.

Phenytoin sodium:

Generic: 100 mg.

Dilantin® (Parke-Davis): Capsules 30 mg and 100 mg.

Phenytoin solution:
Generic: Solution 50 mg/mL in propylene glycol 40%, alcohol 10%, pH adjusted to 11-12.

Fosphenytoin solution:
Cerebyx® 75 mg/mL (equivalent to 50 mg/mL of phenytoin) in 2-mL and 5-mL vials.

Adverse Reactions and Precautions. Phenytoin produces little or no sedation, but at higher blood levels may be associated with blurred or double vision or unsteadiness.

Skin rashes occur in about 8% of patients but are rarely serious. Mild gingival hyperplasia (overgrowth of gums) may be seen in 20% to 50% of patients. Scrupulous oral hygiene prevents inflammation, and severe hyperplasia is uncommon.

Rare but serious reactions involving the bone marrow or liver can also occur. These often disappear after therapy is discontinued but rarely are fatal.

Drug Interactions. Phenytoin may decrease the blood levels of carbamazepine, valproate, ethosuximide, and primidone. Drugs that significantly increase the blood levels of phenytoin include chloramphenicol, cimetidine, dicumarol, disulfiram, isoniazid, sulfonamides, and trimethoprim. Amiodarone, allopurinol, chlorpheniramine, and trazodone may possibly increase the phenytoin levels. Folic acid, prolonged ingestion of alcohol, and rifampin may decrease phenytoin levels. In patients with tuberculosis, the effects of rifampin and isoniazid may cancel each other when these drugs are used with phenytoin. Certain antineoplastic agents (bleomycin, cisplatin, vinblastine) may also reduce blood levels of phenytoin.

Phenytoin may decrease the effectiveness of oral anticoagulants, certain antibiotics (doxycycline, rifampin, and chloramphenicol), oral contraceptives, antiarrhythmic agents (disopyramide, mexiletine, quinidine) digitoxin, analgesics (meperidine, methadone), cyclosporine, corticosteroids, and theophylline. Phenytoin has been reported to impair blood pressure control by dopamine and to decrease the response to skeletal muscle relaxants. So, whenever a new medicine is being considered, ask your physician if it can affect or be affected by phenytoin.

Valproate: Actions and Uses

Valproate (valproic acid [Depakene®] and divalproex sodium [Depakote®]) control absence, myoclonic, and tonic seizures in generalized, idiopathic epilepsy. It is most useful in typical absence seizures. Valproate is as effective as ethosuximide in patients with absence seizures alone and is variably effective in atypical absence seizures. Valproate is the drug of choice for patients with both absence and generalized tonic-clonic seizures.

Comparisons of valproate with carbamazepine or phenytoin in the treatment of partial and secondarily generalized seizures indicate that valproate is similarly effective.

Valproate is the drug of choice in myoclonic epilepsy, with or without generalized tonic-clonic seizures that begin in adolescence or early adulthood. Valproate usually controls photosensitive myoclonus and is also effective in the treatment of benign myoclonic epilepsy, postanoxic myoclonus, and, with clonazepam, in severe progressive myoclonic epilepsy that is characterized by tonic-clonic seizures. It also may be preferred in certain stimulus-sensitive (reflex, startle) epilepsies.

Although valproate may be effective for infantile spasms, it generally should not be used in children whose spasms are caused by hyperglycinemia or other underlying metabolic abnormalities.

In general, atonic and akinetic seizures in patients with Lennox-Gastaut syndrome are difficult to control, but valproate is an effective drug of choice for treatment of these mixed seizure types.

Valproic acid (Depakene®) is absorbed rapidly and completely in the stomach after oral administration; peak blood levels usually occur within 2 hours. The delayed-release tablet preparation, divalproex sodium (Depakote®), reaches peak blood levels 3 to 6 hours after ingestion. A slow-release form (Depakote® Sprinkle) is also available.

Dosage and Administration. Oral: Adults, initially 5 to 15 mg/kg/day; usual maintenance dose, 15 to 25 mg/kg/day.

When used with other AEDs, the initial dose is 10 to 30 mg/kg/day, and the usual maintenance dose is 30 to 60 mg/kg/day.

Children 1 to 12 years, initially, 10 to 30 mg/kg/day; maintenance dose 20 to 30 mg/kg/day. When used with other AEDs, the initial dose is 15 to 45 mg/kg/day and the usual maintenance dose is 30 to 100 mg/kg/day. With polytherapy, some pediatric patients may require more than 100 mg/kg/day to reach effective drug levels. Depakote® Sprinkle may be better for use in children and elderly patients because it is more palatable than the syrup and can be sprinkled over food.

Dosing schedules for the elderly have not been well established, but lower doses may be needed because of slower liver metabolism.

Depakene® Syrup may be given by nasogastric tube.

Intravenous: An IV form of valproic acid is now available (Depacon™). It is intended as replacement therapy for persons unable to take valproate orally.

Valproic Acid:

Generic: capsules 250 mg

Depakene® (Abbott), capsules 250 mg; syrup 250 mg/5 mL

Divalproex Sodium:

Depakote® (Abbott), tablets (delayed-release) 125, 250, and 500 mg.

Depakote® Sprinkle (Abbott), capsules 125 mg.

Adverse Reactions and Precautions. Adverse reactions generally appear early in the course of therapy and are mild and temporary.

The incidence of gastrointestinal (GI) disturbances (nausea, vomiting, anorexia, heartburn) ranges from 6% to 45%. Symptoms are temporary and rarely require drug withdrawal. GI discomfort may be diminished by administering the delayed-release preparation (Depakote® or Depakote® Sprinkle). Diarrhea, abdominal cramps, and constipation are reported occasionally. Increased appetite with weight gain is common and may be controlled by diet, but in some cases, excessive weight gain may require withdrawal of valproate.

Hand tremor is the most common neurologic side effect and occasionally is severe enough to interfere with writing. Tremor occurs more frequently with high doses and may improve with a reduction in dosage.

Sedation and drowsiness develop infrequently in patients receiving valproate alone. Conversely, central nervous system stimulation and excitement have been observed, and aggressiveness and hyperactivity are sometimes noted in children.

Hair loss, thinning, or changes in hair texture occur in some patients, but these effects usually are temporary and do not require the withdrawal of the drug.

Patients should not receive other drugs that affect blood coagulation, including aspirin. A few cases of severe or fatal pancreatitis have been reported. This complication is accompanied by severe abdominal pain and vomiting.

Temporary elevations of liver enzymes are common but not usually related to serious liver dysfunction, and levels often return to normal with or without dosage adjustment. However, fatal liver toxicity has occurred during valproate therapy. Muscle weakness, lethargy, anorexia, and vomiting are often present. Liver toxicity usually develops after an average of 2 months (range, 3 days to 6 months) of therapy.

Guidelines for valproate recommended by the American Academy of Pediatrics and others include:

(1) Avoid giving valproate with other drugs in children under 3 years of age unless monotherapy has failed to control seizures.

(2) Use other effective therapy initially when possible (eg, in absence and febrile seizures), although valproate is effective in many of these and other types of seizures.

(3) Avoid giving valproate to patients with pre-existing liver disease or with family history of childhood liver disease or to critically ill children and children receiving other medication that affects blood coagulation.

(4) Make sure liver function is tested before therapy, 3 to 5 weeks after start of treatment, approximately monthly during the first 6 months of use, and periodically thereafter.

(5) Patients and their parents must report symptoms, such as loss of appetite, lethargy, nausea, vomiting, abdominal pain, jaundice, edema, easy bruising, and loss of seizure control, because laboratory monitoring alone may be inadequate to diagnose valproate-induced liver toxicity. However, if laboratory tests indicate clinically important liver dysfunction, discontinuation of the drug should be considered.

(6) Maintain dosage at the lowest amount that produces the best seizure control.

Drug Interactions. Phenobarbital blood levels may increase by 25% to 68% when valproate is added. This can cause marked sedation or intoxication. Therefore, a 30% to 75% reduction in phenobarbital dosage is required when valproate is added to a patient's drug regimen.

The interaction between valproate and phenytoin is complex. Total phenytoin blood levels may decrease by about 30% during the first several weeks of therapy, but usually do not result in recurrence of seizures because the unbound (free) phenytoin concentration does not change.

Clonazepam: Actions and Uses

Clonazepam (Klonopin®) may be useful alone or in combination with other drugs to control myoclonic or atonic seizures and photosensitive epilepsy. In patients with juvenile myoclonic epilepsy, clonazepam may help control myoclonic jerks but it has not been shown to be useful for the treatment of generalized tonic-clonic seizures. Clonazepam is well absorbed and its peak blood levels occur 1 to 4 hours after oral administration.

Dosage and Administration. Oral: Adults, initially 1.5 mg daily in 3 divided doses, increased by 0.5 to 1 mg every third day until seizures are adequately controlled or until unpleasant side effects occur.

Children, doses of 0.5 mg should be used initially.

Doses for the elderly have not been well established.

Klonopin® (Roche), tablets 0.5, 1, and 2 mg.

Adverse Reactions and Precautions. The most common adverse effects of clonazepam involve the central nervous system. Approximately one half of patients experience drowsiness, about one third ataxia, and up to one quarter personality changes. The sedation may be minimized by starting therapy with a small dose and increasing the amount gradually.

Drug Interactions. Interactions between clonazepam and other AEDs usually are not significant.

Diazepam: Actions and Uses

Intravenous diazepam (Valium®) is effective in continuous tonic-clonic status epilepticus. Its duration of action is short because of its rapid redistribution from the brain. A loading dose of IV phenytoin sodium should be given concomitantly or immediately after control of seizures is achieved with diazepam to maintain antiepileptic activity. Maintenance therapy with oral diazepam is not useful in treating epilepsy.

Rectal administration of the parenteral solution of diazepam is effective for the short-term prevention of acute repetitive seizures and febrile convulsions.

Diazepam's onset of action is almost immediate after IV use. Rapid redistribution from the brain occurs within 30 minutes after injection.

Dosage and Administration. Intravenous: Adults, 5 to 10 mg initially; then as needed to control seizures.

Intravenous: Children, 0.5 mg, followed by 0.25 mg/kg as needed.

Intravenous: Elderly, 5 mg cautiously, with subsequent doses based on the patient's response.

Rectally: Children, 0.5 to 0.8 mg for children under 3 years of age; 0.6 to 0.9 mg for children over 3 years of age.

Generic: solution 5 mg/mL in 1-mL, 2-mL, and 10-mL containers.

Valium® (Roche), solution 5 mg/mL in 2-mL and 10-mL containers.

Rectal Diastat® (Elan), rectal delivery system, 2.5 mg, 5 mg, and 10 mg for children, and 10 mg, 15 mg, and 20 mg for adults.

Adverse Reactions and Precautions. When diazepam is given parenterally for the treatment of status epilepticus, the patient must be observed for signs of respiratory and central nervous system depression and hypotension. This is especially true when diazepam is given with other antiepileptic agents.

Ethosuximide: Actions and Uses

Ethosuximide (Zarontin®) is the drug of choice for absence seizures unaccompanied by other types of seizures. Ethosuximide is more effective and less likely to produce drowsiness and gastrointestinal upset than its chemical relatives.

Ethosuximide also may be effective in myoclonic seizures and akinetic epilepsy, but it is generally ineffective in complex partial or generalized tonic-clonic seizures.

Ethosuximide is well absorbed orally, and the peak blood levels occur in 1 to 4 hours. Control of absence seizures usually is achieved with blood levels of 40 to 100 mg/L, but higher concentrations may be required and tolerated.

Dosage and Administration. Oral: Adults and children over 6 years of age, initially 500 mg daily, increased if necessary by 250 mg every 4 to 7 days until seizures are controlled or until unpleasant side effects develop. The daily maintenance dose is usually 15 to 40 mg/kg.

Children 3 to 6 years of age, initially 250 mg daily with incremental increases in dosage, as for older patients. The daily maintenance dose is usually 15 to 40 mg/kg.

Zarontin® (Parke-Davis), capsules 250 mg; syrup 250 mg/5 mL.

Adverse Reactions and Precautions. The most common adverse reactions to ethosuximide are gastrointestinal disturbances such as nausea and vomiting.

Drug Interactions. Ethosuximide does not consistently change the blood levels of other AEDs.

Phenobarbital: Actions and Uses

Phenobarbital (phenobarbital sodium), a long-acting barbiturate, is effective in generalized tonic-clonic and simple partial seizures. Phenobarbital frequently is used to treat neonatal seizures and may be the initial drug used in young children. However, because of increasing concern about adverse sedative-hypnotic reactions, many physicians prefer less sedating drugs. Thus, phenobarbital is now used less frequently in the United States. It is by far the least expensive medicine, however, and is widely used throughout the world except in Europe and Japan.

Phenobarbital is almost completely absorbed orally, but 1 to 6 hours may be necessary to achieve peak blood levels. The drug also is well absorbed after intramuscular injection.

Dosage and Administration. Oral: Adults, 120 to 250 mg; alternatively, 2 to 3 mg/kg/day. The elderly may need lower doses. Children, 30 to 100 mg daily; these amounts are taken at bedtime. Administration more than once a day is unnecessary.

Parenteral: Both intramuscular and IV administration are well tolerated. It may be given by nasogastric tube. However, rapid IV administration may cause sedation.

Rectal: Phenobarbital solution is well absorbed after rectal administration.

Generic: elixir 15 and 20 mg/mL; tablets 8, 15, 30, 60, and 100 mg; solution.

Adverse Reactions and Precautions. Phenobarbital is associated with significant behavioral and subtle cognitive effects. Drowsiness is the most common side effect, although tolerance usually develops and a significant percentage of patients continue to experience sedation. Furthermore, phenobarbital may affect memory, perceptual motor performance, and tasks requiring sustained performance. Phenobarbital markedly influences behavior; it can provoke irritability and worsen existing behavioral problems, particularly hyperkinesia (excessive activity). A substantial number of adults who take phenobarbital develop mental depression. Phenobarbital must be used cautiously in the elderly because of its tendency to cause sedation, depression, and mental slowing. These side effects may either aggravate existing symptoms of declining brain function or may be confused for the onset of dementia. Abrupt termination of phenobarbital therapy may aggravate seizures, but drug dependence is unlikely with usual antiepileptic doses.

Drug Interactions. Phenobarbital may decrease the clinical effectiveness of oral anticoagulants, oral contraceptives, anti-infectives (chloramphenicol, doxycycline, griseofulvin), some beta-blockers (eg, propranolol, metoprolol), corticosteroids, cyclosporine, some antidepressants (eg, desipramine, nortriptyline), haloperidol, phenothiazines, quinidine, theophylline, digitoxin, doxorubicin, and verapamil.

Primidone: Actions and Uses

Primidone (Mysoline®) is closely related chemically to the barbiturates. Primidone is used principally in generalized tonic-clonic and complex and simple partial seizures. It is as effective as carbamazepine or phenytoin in controlling partial or generalized tonic-clonic seizures, although its greater incidence of side effects limits patient acceptance.

Primidone is rapidly and completely absorbed after oral administration; peak blood levels are attained in an average of 4 hours.

Dosage and Administration. Oral: Adults and older children, initially 125 mg at bedtime for 3 days, with the dose increased by 125 mg every 3 days until a maintenance dose of 250 mg 3 times a day is established on the 10th day.

Children under 8 years of age, initially one half of the adult dosage. For maintenance, 125 mg to 250 mg is given 3 times a day.

Generic: tablets 250 mg

Mysoline® (Elan Pharma), suspension 250 mg/5 mL; tablets 50 and 250 mg.

Adverse Reactions and Precautions. Sedation is common but often diminishes with continued use.

Acetazolamide: Action and Uses

Acetazolamide (AK-Zol®, Diamox®) has been used in absence, generalized tonic-clonic, and partial seizures. It is most often used as an adjunct to other drugs, but its usefulness is limited by the rapid development of tolerance in some patients. Acetazolamide is most widely used in women whose seizure frequency increases with menstruation.

Dosage and Administration. Oral: Adults and children, 8 to 30 mg/kg daily in divided doses (range, 250 mg to 1 g daily).

Generic: tablets 250 mg

AK-Zol® (Akorn), tablets 250 mg.

Newer Antiepileptic Drugs

Eight drugs have been approved since 1993 (Table 2), while a number of other AEDs are still in clinical trials.

Gabapentin: Action and Uses

Gabapentin (Neurontin®, Parke-Davis) is an amino acid. In a U.S. study, 306 patients with partial epilepsy that did not respond to other drugs received doses of 600, 1,200, or 1,800 mg/day. A decrease in seizures was observed at the higher doses. In clinical use, doses of 2,400 to 6,000 mg/day have been used and are well tolerated.

Table 2: Newer Antiepileptic Drugs

Name	Approved Daily Dose	Significant Drug Interactions
Gabapentin (Neurontin®)	900-1,800 mg* in adults	None
Lamotrigine (Lamictal®)	150-600 mg in adults	Valproate increases lamotrigine levels
Felbamate (Felbatol®)	1,800-3,600 mg in adults; 15-45 mg/kg in children	Felbamate increases phenytoin and valproate levels
Topiramate (Topamax®)	400 mg in 2 divided doses	Phenytoin and carbamazepine decrease topiramate levels
Tiagabine (Gabitril®)	Up to 56 mg/day; lower doses if on no inducers	Phenytoin and carbamazepine decrease tiagabine levels
Oxcarbazepine (Trileptal®)	1,200-2,400 mg in adults	Increases phenytoin levels
Zonisamide (Zonegran™)	400-600 mg in adults	Other drugs may decrease its levels
Levetiracetam (Keppra™)	1,000-3,000 mg in adults; 20-40/mg/kg/day in children	None

* Doses as high as 6,000 mg/day have been used and 2,400 to 3,600 mg/day are well tolerated.

Long-term studies of gabapentin have shown that it is well tolerated and does not lose its effectiveness over time. The FDA has approved gabapentin for use in adults as an add-on therapy for partial and secondarily generalized seizures. Its major difference from other antiepileptic medications is its lack of interactions with other drugs. The use of gabapentin in children with epilepsy has been studied and been shown to be well tolerated. Since its introduction for use in epilepsy, gabapentin has been shown to be effective in certain chronic pain syndromes but this is not an approved use by the FDA.

The age group in which gabapentin may be most useful is the elderly. These patients are most likely to be on many other drugs, and gabapentin may be the best tolerated and least problematic.

The time to maximum concentration of gabapentin is 2 to 4 hours after a dose is taken.

Doses. The initial dose of gabapentin in adults is 900 mg/day in divided doses. It can be rapidly titrated, 300 mg on day 1, 300 mg twice a day on day 2, and then 300 mg 3 times a day. Doses of 6,000 mg/day have been well tolerated in adults.

Adverse Reactions and Precautions. The most common side effects from gabapentin are mild fatigue and dizziness. Other side effects have been nystagmus, hypotension (low blood pressure), diarrhea, muscle weakness, dry mouth, sleep disturbances, slurred speech, decreased alertness, tremor, rash, and nausea.

Gabapentin in very large doses appears to have little toxicity; 1 patient took 48 g in an attempted suicide. Even though blood levels were initially over 60 mg/mL, clearance was rapid and she experienced minimal symptoms.

Drug Interactions. The major feature of gabapentin is its lack of interaction with other drugs. Unlike most other

AEDs, gabapentin is not metabolized by the liver. It is almost completely eliminated by the kidneys, so it does not affect the concentrations of the other AEDs, and may have few interactions with other drugs as well. It is especially useful in patients who are receiving many other medications, such as the elderly.

Gabapentin: Neurontin® gelatin capsules, 100, 300, 400 mg.

Lamotrigine: Action and Uses

Lamotrigine (Lamictal®, Glaxo Wellcome) is effective in adults with partial and generalized seizures. It was approved for use for adults with complex partial seizures and secondarily generalized seizures. The use of lamotrigine in children with epilepsy has been studied.

Lamotrigine is rapidly absorbed after oral dosing. In clinical practice, effective serum concentrations of lamotrigine vary from 2 to 20 mg/L.

Doses. Doses of 75 to 600 mg/day have been used in studies of adults with epilepsy. The actual doses used may depend on the tolerance level of each patient. The initial doses of lamotrigine must be adjusted to other medications the patient is taking. If the patient is on an AED other than valproate, the dose should be 50 mg/day for 2 weeks, then 100 mg for the next 2 weeks, and then the dose can be increased by 100 mg each week to a dose of 300 to 500 mg/day. If the patient is on valproate, the initial dose should be 25 mg every other day for 2 weeks, then 25 mg/day for the next 2 weeks, then increased by 25 to 50 mg every week or 2 to a dose of 100 to 150 mg/day.

Adverse Reactions. The most frequently reported side effects of lamotrigine have been double vision, drowsiness, uncoordinated movements (ataxia), and headache. A higher incidence of skin rash has occurred in patients also receiving valproic acid. In children, a high rate of serious skin rashes, including Stevens-Johnson syndrome, has occurred. The manufacturer added a warning that the rate of serious rash may occur in 1 in 50 to 1 in 100 children. Therefore, lamotrigine must be used cautiously in children.

Drug Interactions. Lamotrigine does not appear to affect the blood levels of other AEDs. However, other drugs affect lamotrigine. Phenytoin and carbamazepine significantly shorten lamotrigine's half-life.

Lamotrigine: Lamictal® tablets, 25, 100, 150, 200 mg.

Felbamate: Actions and Uses

Felbamate (Felbatol®, Wallace Laboratories) is effective in adults with partial and generalized seizures. Felbamate has also been shown to reduce atonic seizures and to improve children with Lennox-Gastaut syndrome. The FDA granted approval of felbamate for both add-on therapy and as monotherapy in adults with partial seizures with or without generalization and in children with partial and generalized seizures associated with the Lennox-Gastaut syndrome. But cases of life-threatening aplastic anemia (bone marrow disease) and hepatitis have been reported. Most of the patients developing aplastic anemia had a history of aplastic anemia from other drugs or had a history of immune disorders. Physicians and patients must read the most current warning in the package insert before using this drug. Because of its association with aplastic anemia, felbamate should be reserved for those patients for whom there is no other effective alternative treatment.

The time to maximum blood levels occurs 1 to 4 hours after a dose is administered.

Doses. In adults, doses during clinical trials have ranged from 1,800 to 4,800 mg/day. In children, doses of 15 to

45 mg/kg have been used. With monotherapy, larger doses are tolerated.

Adverse Reactions and Toxicity. No major adverse events were noted during the clinical trials involving more than 2,000 patients. However, after use exceeded 100,000 patients, the high incidence of bone marrow and liver failure became apparent. Monitoring of laboratory tests monthly during the first year and then quarterly is recommended for those patients needing felbamate for epilepsy that does not respond to other drugs. Other side effects include insomnia (sleeplessness), weight loss, nausea, decreased appetite, dizziness, fatigue, imbalance, and tiredness. There were substantially higher rates of side effects in persons receiving other antiepileptic medications.

Drug Interactions. Felbamate has significant interactions with phenytoin, carbamazepine, and valproate. The concentrations of phenytoin and valproate increase with felbamate. Therefore, when felbamate is used, the doses of these other agents should be decreased by 20% to 40% or more. On the other hand, carbamazepine concentrations decrease by about 20% when felbamate is added to therapy. The concentrations of felbamate are lowered by the concomitant use of other AEDs, especially those that induce liver enzymes.

Felbamate: Felbatol® tablets, 400 mg, 600 mg; oral suspension 600 mg/5 mL.

Topiramate: Action and Uses

Topiramate (Topamax®, Ortho-McNeil Pharmaceutical) is approved for use as add-on treatment for adults with partial onset seizures. Absorption is rapid, with peak blood levels occurring in 2 hours.

Doses. In clinical trials of doses of 200, 400, 600, and 1,000 mg per day, there did not appear to be an increase of effectiveness at the higher doses, but side effects were more common. The recommended daily dose for adults is 400 mg in 2 divided doses. Therapy should be initiated at 25 mg/day to 50 mg/day and increased by 25-mg to 50-mg increments.

Adverse Reactions and Toxicity. The most common adverse reactions are somnolence (sleepiness), dizziness, ataxia, speech disorders, psychomotor slowing, and paresthesias. Kidney stones occurred in approximately 1.5% of patients during clinical trials.

Drug Interactions. Topiramate does not appear to affect levels of other drugs. However, phenytoin and carbamazepine decrease topiramate concentrations by 48% and 40%, respectively.

Topiramate: Topamax® tablets, 25, 100, 200 mg.

Tiagabine: Action and Uses

Tiagabine (Gabitril®, Abbott Laboratories) has been found effective for the treatment of partial seizures. It was approved for use as adjunctive therapy in adults and children 12 years and older in the treatment of partial seizures. Absorption is rapid, with peak blood levels occurring approximately 45 minutes after an oral dose.

Doses. In adults, tiagabine should be initiated at 4 mg once a day, increased by 4 to 8 mg at weekly intervals, up to 56 mg per day. Higher doses have been used in some patients, especially those who are receiving other drugs that stimulate liver metabolism.

Adverse Reactions and Toxicity. The most common side effects are somnolence, dizziness, and difficulty with concentration. No systematic abnormalities were found on routine laboratory tests and no specific recommendations regarding routine monitoring have been made. Patients with a history of spike-wave abnormalities on EEG may experience a worsening of those abnormalities as well as clinical symptoms of lethargy or poor responsiveness.

Drug Interactions. Tiagabine has been shown not to have an effect on most drugs, including oral contraceptives. However, drugs that induce hepatic metabolism, especially phenytoin, phenobarbital, and carbamazepine, significantly increase the metabolism of tiagabine and lead to the need for higher doses.

Tiagabine: 4-mg, 12-mg, 16-mg, and 20-mg tablets.

Oxcarbazepine: Actions and Uses

Oxcarbazepine (Trileptal®) is recommended as adjunctive treatment in partial seizures in adults and as adjunctive treatment for partial seizures in children aged 4 to 16. Oxcarbazepine is completely absorbed within an average of 4.5 hours.

Dosage and Administration. As monotherapy, treatment with oxcarbazepine should be initiated with a dose of 300 mg twice a day in adults, and increased by 300 mg every third day to a dose of 1,200 mg/day. As adjunctive therapy, treatment can be initiated at 300 mg twice daily and increased as needed. To convert to monotherapy, other AEDs can then be decreased over 3 to 6 weeks, or longer, as clinically indicated. In general, 300 mg of oxcarbazepine is equivalent to 200 mg of carbamazepine. For children, initial doses should be 8 to 10 mg/kg/day twice a day. Doses can be increased to 20 to 40 mg/kg/day. Children under 8 years of age may need doses 30% to 40% greater.

Adverse Reactions and Precautions. Like carbamazepine, oxcarbazepine may be associated with hyponatremia (a less than normal amount of sodium in the blood). In placebo-controlled studies, 38 of 1,524 (2.5%) patients treated with oxcarbazepine had serum sodium concentrations of less than 125 mmol/L compared to none treated with placebo. In addition, 25% to 30% of patients who had a hypersensitivity reaction to carbamazepine developed a similar reaction to oxcarbazepine. Most common side effects are related to the central nervous system, and include dizziness, somnolence, double vision, fatigue, and ataxia.

Drug Interactions. Oxcarbazepine may increase phenytoin concentrations and may render hormonal contraceptives less effective.

Generic: none

Trileptal®: tablets 150 mg, 300 mg, 600 mg

Zonisamide: Action and Uses

Zonisamide (Zonegran™) is recommended as adjunctive treatment for partial seizures in adults and children (over 12 years of age). It has been available in Japan for more than 10 years, and the experience there suggests it can be effective for certain myoclonic syndromes.

Dosage and Administration. Zonisamide can be started as 100 mg to 200 mg/day in adults, and 2 to 4 mg/kg/day in children. Steady state is reached in 7 to 10 days, and doses can be increased at 2-week intervals. Maintenance doses are 400 to 600 mg/day in adults and 4 to 8 mg/kg/day in children.

Adverse Reactions and Precautions. The most serious adverse event is the development of significant kidney stones in approximately 1.5% of persons in clinical trials in the United States. Interestingly, kidney stones have not been observed in Japan. Other adverse effects include somnolence, ataxia, anorexia, confusion, fatigue, and dizziness.

Drug Interactions. Zonisamide does not induce hepatic enzymes and thus does not appear to affect the metabolism of other drugs. However, in patients receiving either phenytoin or carbamazepine, the half-life of zonisamide was observed to be approximately 30 hours. Lamotrigine may inhibit the clearance of zonisamide.

Zonegran™: tablets 100 mg

Levetiracetam: Actions and Uses

Levetiracetam (Keppra™, UCB Pharma) is indicated for use as adjunctive treatment of partial onset seizures in adults with epilepsy. Its precise mechanism of action is unknown. Levetiracetam is rapidly absorbed in the blood and is the most water soluble drug for epilepsy.

Dosage and Administration. Initial adult doses of levetiracetam are 500 mg twice daily. Clinical studies have shown 1,000 mg/day to be effective. Doses may be increased in increments of 1,000 mg/day. The maximum recommended dose is 3,000 mg/day. Pediatric doses appear to be in the range of 20 to 40 mg/kg/day. In elderly patients and others with decreased kidney function, doses may need to be reduced.

Adverse Reactions and Precautions. In placebo-controlled studies, dizziness, somnolence, and lack of energy were the most commonly reported side effects.

Drug Interactions. Levetiracetam is not metabolized by the liver, and so is not expected to be involved in any drug interactions. No interactions between levetiracetam and phenytoin, warfarin, digoxin, and oral contraceptives have been found by clinical studies.

Generic: none

Keppra™: tablets 250 mg, 500 mg, 750 mg

When Your Doctor Prescribes an Antiepileptic Drug

Once you have started taking a certain brand of medicine, you should not switch to another brand or to a generic version without your doctor's knowledge. This is because AEDs have a narrow therapeutic range, that is, the effective level is close to the toxic level. This is especially true for phenytoin (Dilantin®), for which a 15% difference in the amount absorbed can be the difference between lack of control or toxicity.

When you are on medication for epilepsy, it is very important that you take your pills regularly. We recommend that patients use a pill box that carries an entire week's supply. As soon as you realize that you have missed a dose, you should take it. The most common reason for a seizure to recur is missed medicine. Many medicines stay in the body for only a half day, so it essential to replace the medicine that is missed on schedule.

You should always know the name and prescribed dose of your antiepileptic medicine. Many medicines (including over-the-counter and 'natural' products) can interfere with your epilepsy drugs. Any physician whom you consult needs to know which medicines you are taking so that you can avoid drug interactions. For example, erythromycin, a standard antibiotic commonly used for respiratory tract infections, can triple the level of carbamazepine and cause major side effects.

Treating Epilepsy in the Elderly

Among persons 65 years and older, the active epilepsy prevalence rate is 1.5%, about twice the rate of younger adults. Stroke is the most common identifiable cause of epilepsy in the elderly. Other major causes include brain tumor, head injury, and Alzheimer's disease. In many cases, the cause of epilepsy is never identified. As the elderly population continues to grow, more of them are likely to receive AEDs.

Although the diagnosis of epilepsy is usually made only after a person has had 2 or more seizures, many doctors begin treatment after a single seizure in elderly patients.

This is because there is a good chance a second seizure will occur, especially if there is indication that the person has suffered a stroke, or has a tumor, or malformation in the veins and arteries of the brain. Finding a safe, effective AED can be more difficult for the elderly for a number of reasons:

- They may experience more side effects.
- The signs and symptoms of AED toxicity can be attributed to other causes, such as Alzheimer's disease or stroke, or to other medications they are taking.
- They have a greater risk of drug interactions.
- They may be less able to afford medication.
- Their seizures are sometimes difficult to observe.
- They may not be able to accurately report their problems.

Deciding When to Stop Treatment

In the past, many experts advised that treatment could stop after a patient had been free of seizures for 2 years. Based on what we have learned about epileptic syndromes in recent years, this recommendation is no longer considered valid. As stressed before, *you should never discontinue AED treatment without first discussing it with your doctor.*

Like the decision to start treatment, the decision to stop treatment must be made based on the probability of recurrent seizures. Some epileptic syndromes are age-specific, and some patients mature to the stage of low risk. For other syndromes, there is a lifelong tendency for seizures to occur, and the fact that these seizures are controlled does not mean that the disorder responsible for causing them is in remission. In recent studies, the factors found to be related to successful withdrawal of medication were: a single type of seizure; normal neurologic examination;

normal IQ; and normal EEG following treatment. Any decision to stop treatment must be made with an understanding of the risks involved.

It's important to understand that medication should never be stopped abruptly because it may lead to withdrawal seizures. If you and your doctor decide to stop treatment, the medication should be tapered over a period of weeks or months, depending on its characteristics. Phenobarbital, in particular, has great potential for causing withdrawal seizures and should be withdrawn over a period of months.

Case Reports

Case report 1. The parents of a 7-year-old girl heard disturbing noises from her bedroom at 2 AM. They rushed in and saw the girl having what was later diagnosed as a generalized tonic-clonic seizure. The took her to a hospital emergency room. The girl was awake, but sleepy, and was sent home with an appointment for an EEG and a visit with a neurologist. The EEG showed the characteristic pattern of benign rolandic epilepsy. The neurologist recommended no treatment.

Case report 2. A 10-year-old boy had a generalized tonic-clonic seizure at school. He recovered in a hospital emergency room and was sent home. An EEG done a week later was normal, but physicians learned, by taking a patient history, that the boy had had a serious head injury 3 years earlier. The decision was made not to begin treatment with AEDs. However, 5 years later, the boy had a second seizure, and drug treatment was started. Carbamazepine was initially chosen, but the boy developed a rash. Phenytoin was then used and the patient has been seizure-free.

Case report 3. A 17-year-old girl had a generalized tonic-clonic seizure at home at night. An EEG was normal. She was started on carbamazepine but had seizures 6 months and 9 months later. She was referred to a neurologist, who found out through a patient history that since she was 15 the girl had been having sudden involuntary movements ('jerks') in the mornings. Another EEG showed the characteristic pattern of juvenile myoclonic epilepsy.

Valproate was substituted for carbamazepine and both the generalized tonic-clonic seizure seizures and the myoclonic movements ('jerks') came under control. At 22 she wanted to start a family but valproate has an additional risk of 1% to 2% for birth defects. After careful consideration, she decided to continue the valproate while trying to get pregnant because the medicine had controlled her seizures so well and seizures during pregnancy are more damaging than the medicines.

Case report 4. A 37-year-old man had a generalized tonic-clonic seizure. An MRI showed a small glial (benign) tumor in the right temporal lobe. He was started on phenytoin, which controlled the generalized seizures, but he then began to suffer complex partial seizures. Carbamazepine was added to his medicine but he developed unsteadiness.

Lamotrigine was then substituted, but the complex partial seizures continued. Gabapentin and tiagabine were tried also, but 3 years later the seizures resumed. He was referred to an epileptologist, which is a neurologist who specializes in epilepsy. After considering the options, a temporal lobectomy (surgery) was done. The patient has been free of tonic-clonic seizures, but his periodic EEGs show some spikes. Therefore, he is being maintained on a low dose of phenytoin.

Case report 5. A 72-year-old woman, who had had a stroke a year earlier, was being treated for high blood pressure, diabetes, and a recent herpes zoster infection. Then she suffered a single complex partial seizure. Because of the high risk of additional seizures, gabapentin was started to treat the seizures and also to avoid the interactions with her other medicines.

Chapter 5

Surgical Treatment for Epilepsy

Surgery is an option for treating epilepsy. It was once only used as a last resort, and only after other options failed to control seizures. This often meant patients suffered uncontrolled seizures for years and risked permanent brain damage, serious bodily injury, and difficult psychological and social problems.

Recently, with the development of sophisticated monitoring procedures and noninvasive imaging techniques, surgery has become widely accepted as a treatment for intractable epilepsy. Patients are considered to have intractable epilepsy when their seizures have not been brought under control within 1 year after drug therapy has been started and is documented by checking blood levels. A person with intractable epilepsy should be evaluated by a physician with special expertise in epilepsy.

Although risks exist in all surgical procedures, most brain surgery for epilepsy is safe. The rate of success depends on the type of epilepsy syndrome and it may be predicted after presurgical testing. There are 2 main categories of epilepsy surgery, both of which involve the

brain: removal of the area of the brain that is producing the seizures; and interruption of nerve pathways along which seizure impulses spread. Some types of epilepsy surgery that are available include:
- Lobectomy
- Hemispherectomy
- Corpus callosotomy
- Multiple subpial transection

Lobectomy

Surgical treatment of epilepsy involves identifying and removing the impulse-conducting cells in the brain that cause the seizures. The brain is divided into 4 main areas (see Figure 1, Chapter 1), called lobes, located on each side of the head. They are the temporal lobe, frontal lobe, parietal lobe, and occipital lobe (see Figure 1, Chapter 1). Simple or complex partial seizures begin in 1 or more of these lobes. They can take on different forms, depending on the area of the brain in which they originate. When a person has seizures that start in the same lobe every time, it is sometimes possible to stop the seizures by removing some or all of that lobe, if it can be done without damaging vital functions. The best surgical outcomes, defined as those with the highest cure rates, are seen in people with mesial temporal sclerosis. This syndrome can be diagnosed by epilepsy specialists based on the patient's medical history, special MRI scans, EEG, and neuropsychological testing.

According to the Epilepsy Foundation (EFA), some 65% to 85% of patients who undergo lobectomies will be seizure-free, but serious complications occur in about 4 of every 100 surgeries. Complications vary, based on the kind of surgery, and include: stroke, partial loss of vision, motor ability, memory, or speech; and temporary infection or swelling of the brain.

Hemispherectomy

In rare cases, a child may have severe brain disease on one side of the brain that produces uncontrollable seizures and paralysis on the opposite side of the body. When this occurs, it may require a more extensive operation. Unlike the lobectomy, which removes a fairly small area of the brain, a *hemispherectomy* removes all or almost all of one side (hemisphere) of the brain. It's difficult to believe that a person could function with only half a brain, but in children, the remaining half of the brain takes over some of the functions of the part that was removed. There will be a loss of peripheral (side) vision, and weakness and loss of movement on the opposite side of the body.

The EFA has said that the small number of specialized surgical centers doing hemispherectomies report excellent results. However, there are more risks than with other types of epilepsy surgery. Children who have this operation will continue to experience loss of function on the side of the body opposite the side where the brain was removed.

Corpus Callosotomy

Instead of removing brain tissue, the *corpus callosotomy* interrupts the spread of seizures by cutting the nerve fibers that serve as a bridge connecting one side of the brain to the other. These fibers are called the corpus callosum. The types of seizures that may respond to this surgery include uncontrolled, generalized tonic-clonic (grand mal) seizures, drop attacks, or massive jerking movements. Because these seizures affect both sides of the brain at once, there is usually no one area that can be removed to prevent them. This surgery doesn't usually stop seizure activity completely. Some type of seizure activity is likely to continue on one side of the brain, but it is usually less severe than repeated drop attacks or convulsions.

EFA figures indicate that risks of complications after a corpus callosotomy are 20 per 100 operations. Generalized seizures may decrease or stop, but partial seizures are likely to continue and may get worse. However, the generalized tonic-clonic seizures that the operation is designed to treat are also associated with serious risks. Weighing the risks involved in surgery against the risk of serious injury associated with generalized tonic-clonic seizures is an important decision.

Multiple Subpial Transection

Some seizures begin in or spread to areas of the brain that can't be safely removed because they control critical functions such as movement or language. Because removing these areas could risk paralysis or loss of speech ability, a *multiple subpial transection* (MST) may be recommended. This surgical technique, which may be used alone or in addition to a lobectomy, involves interfering with the spread of seizure impulses by making a small incision in the brain.

Presurgical Evaluation

Surgery is *not* the first choice of treatment for epilepsy. It is usually reserved for patients whose seizures cannot be controlled by antiepileptic medication and who have an epilepsy syndrome for which surgery can be effective, such as mesial temporal sclerosis. When considering surgery, communication between the doctor, the patient, and family members is critical. A number of important factors need to be considered, including:
- How do frequent seizures affect the patient's life-style?

- How likely is it that antiepileptic medication will control seizures?
- What are the side effects of the antiepileptic medication?
- Can the area of the brain causing the seizures be accurately located?
- What risks are associated with the surgery?

The objective of the presurgical evaluation is to identify the area of the brain responsible for recurring seizures and prove that it can be removed without causing unacceptable losses in function. It can be a long and difficult process that begins with long-term monitoring using electroencephalogram (EEG) and video to record the electrical activity and symptoms that occur during an epileptic seizure. Depending on the type of surgery considered, a number of other diagnostic tests may be required, including positron emission tomography (PET) or magnetic resonance imaging (MRI).

In addition to the physical testing, the presurgical evaluation should include an assessment by a neuropsychologist. Because epilepsy affects every aspect of a person's life—including self-image, level of independence, relationships with family and friends, and employability—it's important to consider how surgery might affect the patient's quality of life. For example, a person who was unemployable before surgery needs to understand that there is no guarantee he or she will be employable after the surgery. Also, depending on where the tissue causing the seizures is located, there is some risk that surgery will cause impairment, or loss, of some function. The patient and his or her family need to decide if this functional loss is an acceptable tradeoff for eliminating seizures.

The Operation

Surgery for epilepsy is a complex procedure that should only be performed in a medical center that specializes in this type of surgery. Its success depends on careful selection of patients and the skill and experience of the surgical team. During the surgery, the surgeon may use EEG recordings to map the area of the brain to be removed and may stimulate the brain with mild electrical impulses to identify special areas controlling speech, movement, and sensation.

Recuperation generally involves up to a week of hospitalization and 3 to 8 weeks of continued healing at home before normal activities can be resumed. Doctors usually have patients continue on antiepileptic medication 2 years or more after surgery. To retain seizure control, some people may have to continue taking medication indefinitely.

The cost of surgery for epilepsy can vary greatly. This is because some cases are more challenging than others and may require more testing and evaluation prior to the operation. The EFA cites a range of $35,000 to more than $150,000. This cost is comparable to many commonly performed surgeries such as coronary artery bypass. The cost is covered by most health insurance plans. However, if surgery is successful in completely controlling seizures, it can be very cost effective.

Some Important Considerations

If you or a loved one is considering surgery for epilepsy, you need to communicate openly with your doctor so that you and your family members have a realistic picture of the risks and benefits. With continued improvement in medical technology, surgery for epilepsy is becoming more common, safer, and more successful. However, it is still major surgery with all the accompanying risks. Not all patients are good candidates for surgery, and having the surgery does not guarantee that you will be free of seizures or that you will no longer need to take medication. Still, there is a good chance that you will have fewer seizures and, perhaps, may even become seizure-free.

It's important to understand that there may be some physical after effects and emotional changes following epilepsy surgery. It's not uncommon to feel depressed following any major surgery. You may also feel disappointed if your seizures don't stop entirely or if you have to continue taking antiepileptic medication. In addition, you may find it difficult to adjust to life without seizures and to live up to the expectations of others. These reactions are usually temporary. Anticipating them can help you and your family handle them more constructively.

Chapter 6

Other Treatment Options

The Vagus Nerve Stimulator

The vagus nerve stimulator (VNS) may be a treatment option for people who have epilepsy that does not respond to drugs and who are not good candidates for brain surgery. Approved by the Food and Drug Administration (FDA) in 1997, the vagus nerve stimulator is flat, round, and about the size of a hockey puck. It contains a battery pack, a computer chip, and connecting wire.

The VNS works much like a cardiac pacemaker. It is implanted in the chest under the collar bone and the leads at the end of the connecting wire are attached to the vagus nerve, on the left side of the neck, and runs from the base of the brain into the abdomen (Figure 1). The vagus nerve controls various *autonomic* functions (activities that occur automatically, without conscious thought, such as heart rate and taste).

The doctor programs the VNS to control the strength, duration and frequency of the electrical discharge it produces. Typically, the vagus nerve is stimulated approximately every 5 minutes for about 30 seconds and conducts the electrical charge to the brain where it changes

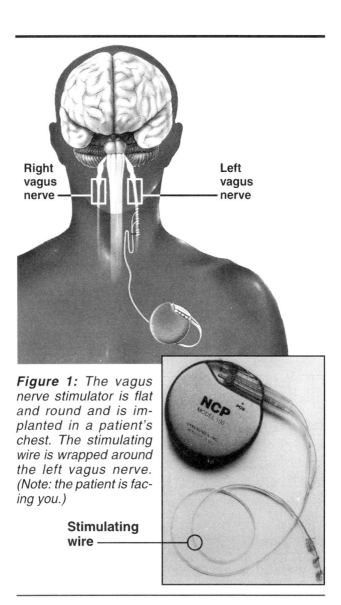

Figure 1: The vagus nerve stimulator is flat and round and is implanted in a patient's chest. The stimulating wire is wrapped around the left vagus nerve. (Note: the patient is facing you.)

the brain's electrical pattern. For some patients, this has the effect of reducing the frequency and severity of seizures. A small number of patients have even become seizure-free. Patients who experience *auras* warning them of an impending seizure can stop or shorten the length of the seizure by activating the VNS. This is done by holding a magnet over the pocket of skin that hides the VNS. Scientists are not sure how this brain stimulation controls seizures, but studies have shown that the VNS is about as effective in reducing seizures as the new antiepileptic drugs (AEDs).

There is no guarantee that the VNS will work for a patient, but it is a promising option for people who experience many seizures a day. The FDA has approved the VNS for adults and adolescents older than 12 years who suffer from partial seizures. Clinical studies indicate that vagus nerve stimulation may also be effective for younger children and people with generalized seizures.

The implant cost of around $18,000 to $22,000, which includes hospitalization, is covered by most insurers. The surgery is minor and relatively free from complications. In rare cases, the patient may become infected and there may be some itching. Brief hoarseness and throat discomfort during the stimulation cycle are the most common side effects.

The Ketogenic Diet

The ketogenic diet is a high-fat, low-protein and carbohydrate diet used to treat difficult-to-control seizures. It is a highly controversial option for treating epilepsy that was originally developed in the 1920s by scientists at the Mayo Clinic and Johns Hopkins University. It was widely used until after World War II when new AEDs were introduced. For the next several decades, interest in the ketogenic diet faded because AEDs were generally much more effective and easier to use than the diet.

However, the ketogenic diet continued to be used by some epilepsy specialists to treat children with intractable epilepsy that did not respond to AEDs. The ketogenic diet has been placed on the FDA list of 'experimental treatments,' centers have been established at medical facilities across the country, and a number of clinical trials have been conducted.

The idea for the ketogenic diet sprang from the observation, over many years, that fasting was an effective way to control seizures. The diet is designed to trick the body into a state of starvation forcing it to use more fat than normal for energy. This results in the production of ketones—hence the name *ketogenic*.

The ketogenic diet has many undesirable side effects, but many of them can be controlled. They include:
- High cholesterol levels
- Constipation
- Deficiency in vitamins B and C, and calcium
- Kidney stones
- Stunted growth
- Acidosis and excess ketosis during illness

On the other hand, the ketogenic diet has fewer effects on mental functioning than AEDs used in high doses. In some children with very difficult-to-treat epilepsy, the ketogenic diet's success rate is better than that with multiple AEDs.

The ketogenic diet is *not* a first-line treatment for epilepsy. It does seem to hold promise for some people, particularly children, who endure multiple daily seizures that can't be controlled by any other means, or who experience debilitating side effects from AEDs. Undertaking the ketogenic diet requires a strong commitment from both the patient and his or her parents or caregivers. Because it is a complicated medical treatment that is highly individualized and strictly controlled, it should not be undertaken without the supervision of experienced medical professionals.

Initiating the diet involves 2 days of fasting during which the child is gradually placed on the special high-fat, low-carbohydrate, low-protein diet with restricted fluid intake. During that time, the parents participate in a teaching program to learn the reasoning behind the diet; how to calculate the meals and weigh the foods; how to read product labels; and how to manage the diet during childhood illnesses. Strict compliance is critical to the success of the ketogenic diet —even taking a vitamin or medication that contains a small amount of sugar can have an adverse effect.

If you want to learn more about the ketogenic diet, it's best to begin by discussing it with your physician. If he or she is unable to satisfactorily answer your questions, information is available through the Charlie Foundation at the following address: 1223 Wilshire Blvd., #815, Santa Monica, CA 90403-5406, 1-800-367-5386

The Internet can also be a good source of information. Using the search term 'ketogenic diet' will access a number of Web sites, but it's important to make sure that the information comes from a reliable source, such as a major teaching hospital or government health care agency.

Natural Products

Many natural chemicals have medicinal properties. Epilepsy patients must be especially careful before using 'natural remedies.' St. John's Wort, which is available over the counter to treat mild depression, contains at least 25 different chemicals that are known to affect the body. Some of these chemicals can excite the nervous system, and there have been reports of people with epilepsy whose seizures worsened after taking St. John's Wort. Similar reports have been made about the weight-loss product Metabolite.

An epilepsy patient should not use natural products unless the product's manufacturer can show evidence that it contains no natural chemicals that excite the nervous system. If patients experience an increase in seizures while using a natural product, they should report it to their physicians as well as to the product's supplier and stop using it.

Many chemicals extracted from natural products appear to offer promise in treating epilepsy. The major difference between natural products and prescription drugs developed from natural chemicals is that prescription drugs have been purified, tested thoroughly, and manufactured to contain a consistent amount of ingredients in each dose.

Research to Control and Cure Epilepsy

Basic research into the mechanisms on how the brain works is leading to advancements in epilepsy treatment. Some developments involve genetic research. Genes have been identified that have very specific programs to form molecules that have a major influence on how the brain works. For example, one gene has been identified that controls the building of the potassium channel, and a defect in this gene has been found in families with certain types of epilepsy. Furthermore, a drug that works on the potassium channel is being developed, and may offer a treatment for this epilepsy syndrome as well as other seizure types.

These and other exciting developments were recently reviewed at a White House-initiated conference on 'Curing Epilepsy' sponsored by the National Institutes of

Health, the American Epilepsy Society, Epilepsy Foundation, Citizens United for Research in Epilepsy, and the National Association of Epilepsy Centers. Information about the conference can be obtained from Director, NINDS, Building 31, Room 8A52, 31 Center Drive, MSC 2540, Bethesda, MD 20892. E-mail: gf33n@nig.gov.

In an effort to educate people affected by epilepsy about genetic research and to enlist families to participate in clinical genetic research projects, the Epilepsy Foundation has initiated The Gene Discovery Project. To find out more about the project, visit the EFA Web site (www.efa.org) or contact it in one of the following ways: write to 4351 Garden City Drive, Landover, Maryland 20785; call them at 1-800-332-1000, fax them at 1-301-577-2684, or e-mail them at info@efa.org.

Research can only move forward if the public supports research efforts. Progress in epilepsy treatment depends on animal research. All new drugs and devices must be first tested on animals for safety and effectiveness; there is no alternative. Once a new drug has passed tests for safety and effectiveness in animals models of epilepsy, the FDA permits a sponsor (the drug company holding the patent) to begin testing in humans. A new drug is tested on a trial group of approximately 2,000 epilepsy patients, and it must be proven to be safe and to perform significantly better than a placebo before it is approved for sale to the public. Of 250 chemicals (natural or synthetic) which show promise in the laboratory, only about 10 pass the animal tests and 5 are approved for use by people. It costs approximately $500 million to bring a drug to market, and drug manufacturers have only 5 to 7 years of exclusive rights to sell the drug. Human testing of epilepsy drugs takes many years. These factors account for why new drugs are so expensive.

Test groups for epilepsy drugs are limited to patients with only epilepsy and no other medical issues, such as diabetes, heart disease, or pregnancy. Drug trial groups are limited to 2,000 participants, so the possibility that unexpected side effects sometimes occur after a drug is on the market should come as no surprise. A side effect that affects 1 in 5,000 people, for example, might not be detected by the present system.

Preventing seizures through electrically stimulating the nervous system is another new direction in therapy being explored. One device, the VNS discussed earlier in this chapter, is already on the market. Direct stimulation of the brain by implanted electrodes is being researched in animals and has been tried in a few humans. This approach may offer great promise in the future. These devices may be able to detect the onset of a seizure and abort it by delivering stimulation to the brain.

Chapter 7

Women and Epilepsy

According to the Epilepsy Foundation (EFA), more than 1 million American women and girls are living with epilepsy. They are faced with a number of problems, including the fact that hormonal changes during the menstrual cycle may trigger seizures. For women and girls with epilepsy, the issues are:

- Seizures often begin in puberty, which can make one of the most difficult times in their lives even more difficult.
- The areas of the brain that are often involved in adult epilepsy are sensitive to the effects of reproductive hormones.
- Seizures and antiepileptic drugs (AEDs) present a number of risks to pregnant women and their babies.
- Seizures that begin with the beginning of menstruation may improve at menopause, or may become worse. No one knows what factors influence either outcome.

Although hormones are an important factor in women's health, there has been little systematic investigation into the role hormones play as a contributing cause of epilepsy or in its treatment. Unfortunately, most of the epilepsy research has involved men. The small amount of research that has been done on women seems to indicate that hormonal swings during the monthly cycles worsen seizures. This is something women have been saying for years.

The EFA has recently begun a campaign to help women with epilepsy. The Women and Epilepsy Initiative hopes to combat the problems of females with epilepsy in 3 ways: targeted research, improved medical care, and increased community understanding. The initiative's 4 primary goals are to: empower women with epilepsy to improve their health care and develop a support network; make health-care providers aware of the difficulties confronting women with epilepsy and improve their quality of care; improve public understanding of epilepsy and its impact on the lives of women and their families, and encourage support for available programs and services; and stimulate scientific interest in the problems of women with epilepsy, solicit support for research into the causes, and, hopefully, find solutions.

Menstruation

Hormonal changes during the menstrual cycle seem to have an effect on seizures. Menstrual periods don't cause seizures but for some women, seizures may worsen or be clustered during the menstrual period. Since seizures are random events, it makes sense that they may occur around a menstrual period just by chance. However, some women seem to experience seizures only, or primarily, during the days just before their menstrual period begins. This is referred to as *catamenial epilepsy*, and often is seen in women who menstruate irregularly or without ovulation. Taking drugs to restore ovulation or regulate the menstrual cycle may improve seizure control for these women, but is not a substitute for antiepileptic medication.

Contraception

None of the available methods of contraception have a significant effect on seizures. However, it's important that women taking an AED who are considering using one of the hormonal methods of birth control inform their neurologist. Certain medications used to control epilepsy can reduce the effect of the hormonal contraceptive and, consequently, increase the chance of becoming pregnant. Common kinds of hormonal contraceptives include:

- Birth control pills
- Contraceptives implanted under the skin (Norplant®)
- Contraceptives implanted in the uterus (IUD Progestasert®)
- Contraceptives given by injection (Depo-Provera®)

Studies have shown that doses of hormonal contraceptives must be increased when women are taking AEDs that speed up the metabolism of birth control pills. These include barbiturates (phenobarbital), phenytoin (Dilantin®), carbamazepine (Tegretol®, Carbatrol®), and valproate (Depacon™ and Depakene®), oxcarbazepine (Trileptal®). Ethosuximide (Zarontin®), levetiracetam (Keppra™), gabapentin (Neurontin®), and lamotrigine (Lamictal®) have the least effect on the metabolism of hormonal contraceptives. To prevent an unwanted pregnancy, it's a good idea to use condoms or a diaphragm during the first month of hormonal contraceptive use.

Pregnancy

As a group, women who have epilepsy have fewer children than women who don't have epilepsy. This may be due to problems caused by seizures; problems with the menstrual cycle and reproductive organs; and fears of having a child with epilepsy, birth defects, or other problems. Sexual disinterest, which can affect both men and women with epilepsy, is another possible factor. Lack of interest in sex could be a side effect of an AED, or it could be because seizures start in the temporal lobe, which is connected to an area of the brain thought to play a role in emotional behavior. In addition, the attitudes of other people discourage many women with epilepsy from becoming pregnant. Despite this, most women with epilepsy are able to conceive and give birth to normal, healthy babies.

Approximately 20,000 births occur among women with epilepsy each year in the United States. Pregnancy raises a number of issues for these women and their physicians, including:

- The effect of pregnancy on seizure frequency
- The effect of seizures on the fetus
- The effect of AEDs on the growth and development of the fetus
- Problems with labor and delivery
- The implications for breast-feeding
- The ability of a mother with seizures to care for her child

It's important that women discuss these concerns with their physicians before conceiving. If a doctor is aware that a woman is trying to conceive, he or she can make decisions accordingly.

Seizure Frequency

Pregnancy is associated with a number of physical, hormonal, and psychological changes that might increase seizure frequency, but the best predictor of seizure frequency during pregnancy is seizure frequency before pregnancy. In 1 study, most patients who had more than 1 seizure per month had an increase in seizures during pregnancy. In contrast, women who averaged fewer than

1 seizure every 9 months did not experience an increase during pregnancy.

Some factors that increase seizures in pregnant women include:
- Poor seizure control before the pregnancy
- Poor compliance with antiepileptic medication
- Lack of sleep due to anxiety and other psychological factors
- Changes in the metabolism of the AED.

The most important step a woman can take to reduce her risk of increased seizures during a pregnancy is to work with her doctor to get her seizures under control before becoming pregnant. Avoiding fatigue, emotional stress, and any other factors that were suspected of playing a role in triggering past seizures can also reduce the risk for increased seizures during pregnancy.

Because levels of AEDs fall during pregnancy, blood levels need to be checked regularly, and the AED dose may be increased to prevent seizures as a pregnancy advances. Patients can help their physicians evaluate the AED levels in the blood by keeping record of seizure frequency and medication intake.

The Effects of Seizures on the Fetus

Many expectant mothers who have seizures have normal babies, but research indicates that seizures during a pregnancy can adversely affect fetal development and cause stillbirth. Experiencing generalized tonic-clonic (grand mal) seizures during pregnancy has not been associated with birth defects. However, they can cause miscarriages, although rarely, and can injure the baby if they occur during the last month of pregnancy. Complex partial seizures may result in accidents or injuries that may harm the mother and indirectly harm the baby if the mother requires extensive treatment, particularly if it involves multiple drugs. For these reasons, it's important that pregnant women work with their doctors to reduce seizures as much as possible.

The Effect of AEDs on the Fetus

Any woman, even if she is healthy, has a 2% to 3% chance of having a baby with a birth defect. That risk rises to 4% to 6% for women with epilepsy. The cause of the increased risk of malformations has been the topic of debate, but there are 3 strong possibilities:
- The birth defects may be genetically related to whatever causes epilepsy.
- The birth defects may be related to the AED(s) used to control seizures.
- The birth defects may occur because the baby has a genetic susceptibility to harmful effects of medications.

The most common types of birth defects occurring in children born to mothers with epilepsy are cleft lip or cleft palate (commonly called a *harelip*) and heart defects. Women who take divalproex (Depakote®, Depacon™, or Depakene®) have a 1% or greater chance that their children will develop spina bifida, a serious defect that affects the lower spinal cord. This is more likely with higher doses. Carbamazepine (Tegretol®) also poses a risk for spina bifida. Other potential defects affect the appearance of the child. They include minor malformations of the face, fingers, and toes, and a smaller-than-average head. One advantage the new drugs offer is that few birth defects have been detected with them during animal testing. This suggests that these drugs may not cause birth defects in humans, but because pregnant women are not eligible to participate in drug testing trials, we have little information now.

Most studies show that the risk of malformations increases with the number of drugs used. The incidence of malformation was the highest in patients who took medicines *and* who had seizures during pregnancy. This suggests that the highest risk of fetal injury occurs in women whose seizures are incompletely controlled even with multiple drug use. Most birth defects caused by drugs occur during the first trimester. For this reason, a woman of childbearing age should question her doctor about a drug's potential for causing birth defects (*teratogenicity*) at the time it is first prescribed. Decisions about which AEDs to use should be made before pregnancy occurs. Stillbirths or miscarriages are more common in women who have epilepsy but the risk varies with the severity of epilepsy.

Labor and Delivery

Although some studies indicate that women with epilepsy are more likely to have some type of intervention during delivery, merely having epilepsy is not a reason for having a cesarean section. Seizures rarely occur during delivery. If a seizure does occur, it can make the delivery more difficult but is usually not dangerous. A frequent problem encountered during labor and delivery is the tendency for bleeding in babies born to mothers who take certain AEDs. This can be prevented by taking vitamin K during the last 2 to 4 weeks of pregnancy.

Some AEDs, particularly phenobarbital, can affect newborn babies. Babies born to mothers who take these medications during pregnancy may seem sedated during the first few hours, or even a few days, after birth. After the sedation wears off, some babies may experience withdrawal symptoms, such as irritability, tremor, vomiting, poor sucking, rapid breathing, and sleep disturbances.

These symptoms usually last a few days. If the symptoms last longer than a few days you should check with your physician.

Some Important Considerations

If you are an expectant mother, you can minimize the risks for you and your baby by doing everything possible to maximize the chances of a normal pregnancy and uncomplicated delivery. The most important thing you can do to assure the health of your baby is to take care of yourself. This includes consulting with your obstetrician early and often; taking prenatal vitamins containing folic acid; getting proper amounts of food, sleep, and exercise; minimizing stress; and avoiding smoking, alcohol, and caffeine. It's also important to maintain regular appointments with your neurologist, who will help monitor your antiepileptic medication as the pregnancy progresses. Any decision to change or discontinue antiepileptic medication should be made by your neurologist. You should never abruptly discontinue an AED.

Breast-Feeding

Breast-feeding is an important concern for women with epilepsy who have babies, because nearly all AEDs are transferred in breast milk, some in smaller amounts than others. Mothers can breast-feed their babies but they need to take certain precautions, especially if they are taking phenobarbital, primidone (Mysoline®), or benzodiazepines (Valium® and lorazepam). These drugs can attain higher levels in breast milk. Babies of mothers who are taking AEDs need to be watched for signs of sedation. If your baby appears to be sedated, or is not gaining weight, you should check with your physician. Remember, the amount of medicine delivered by breast milk is much less than a fetus receives.

Caring for an Infant

It is not unusual for a woman with epilepsy to have a seizure while caring for her baby. One study shows that seizures are more likely to occur in the postpartum period. This isn't surprising because the body has been stressed during labor and delivery, and, with a new baby in the house, it's difficult to find time to rest. Two important things a new mother can do to minimize the risk of a seizure are to take her medication as prescribed by her physician, and enlist the help of a family member or friend to ensure she gets enough rest.

There are a number of precautions you can take to reduce the risk of potential harm for your new baby. If you have a warning before the onset of a seizure, it's a good idea to set up a secure area in each room so you will have a place to safely lay the baby down if you feel a seizure coming on. If you don't experience an immediate warning but feel a bit strange for several hours before a seizure, you may want to ask a friend or family member to stay with you on such days. Here are other precautions you can take to keep your baby safe:

- Change the baby's diapers and clothing on the floor, or, if you use a changing table, make sure you always strap the baby in.
- Always make sure someone else is with you when you give your baby a bath.
- Always strap your baby into an infant seat, even if you intend to stay close by.
- Use a cloth-front baby carrier whenever you are walking or standing and holding your baby. However, this is not a good idea if you suffer from generalized tonic-clonic (grand mal) or other types of seizures that may cause you to fall.

- Use an infant seat or pillows to make a comfortable seat on the floor when feeding your baby.
- Never hold your baby while cooking, ironing, or doing other household chores that could endanger your baby.

Chapter 8

Epilepsy and Quality of Life

Most people with epilepsy are normal except for being at risk for seizures. Seizure and the control of seizures take only a small part of their daily lives, often occurring as infrequently as once every few months or even every few years. Between seizures they can lead normal lives. However, the diagnosis of epilepsy creates major social barriers for many, including the problems associated with medication side effects, the personal fear of losing control, and society's revulsion at seeing a person struggle with a seizure. Although there is still much to learn, the medical profession has come a long way in understanding how to diagnose and treat epilepsy. The public understanding of epilepsy has also improved, but people who have been diagnosed with epilepsy still feel stigmatized and often find themselves being treated differently, and sometimes unfairly.

If you or someone you love has been recently diagnosed with epilepsy, you may already be dealing with quality-of-life issues in one or more of the following areas:
- Employment
- Sports

- Sexuality and interpersonal relations
- Personal safety
- Mental function
- Driving

Understanding what these issues might be and knowing your legal rights can help you face them and deal with them constructively.

Employment

Employment discrimination is one of the biggest problems facing persons with epilepsy. Although they may have average or above-average intelligence and be otherwise healthy, the unpredictable loss of consciousness associated with seizures can make them unsuitable for some jobs. There are no hard-and-fast rules, but it is generally agreed that a person with epilepsy should avoid jobs in which a sudden loss of consciousness might expose him or her, or a coworker, to injury. For example, a person with a history of epilepsy cannot operate interstate trucks even if seizures are controlled. There are also strict regulations that apply to people with epilepsy who want to operate aircraft.

In other jobs that may seem inappropriate for a person with epilepsy, such as working in high places or operating heavy equipment, precautions can be taken that greatly diminish the risk of injury. With proper safety equipment such as a harness, which should be available for all workers, the risk of injury with seizures is significantly reduced. Therefore, a person with epilepsy should not automatically be excluded from working in high places.

The same can be said of operating heavy equipment with proper safety devices. For a farm worker with epilepsy, the tractor should be equipped with a 'dead-man' brake, which shuts the equipment down when the driver loses control. Although there are few office positions that should be denied a person with epilepsy, some employers may be reluctant to hire a person with epilepsy to work in a position that requires him or her to make a good public impression.

Employers' attitudes toward persons with epilepsy have become more favorable in recent years, but some employers still refuse to hire a worker with epilepsy even though the applicant may be qualified for the job. If you think an employer has treated you unfairly, you could have legal recourse through such federal laws as the Americans with Disabilities Act (ADA) and the Rehabilitation Act of 1973, or through antidiscrimination laws in your state. It is always best to seek the advice of an attorney, but if that isn't possible, you always have the option of filing a complaint with the state or federal government. The federal Equal Employment Opportunity Commission (EEOC) has designated certain regional offices to handle complaints related to the ADA.

Sports

Participation in sports is important for many people, particularly students. Unfortunately, many parents and school officials unnecessarily limit the epileptic student's participation in sports because they fear injury. There is little or no evidence that physical fatigue, such as experienced in strenuous activity, will lead to a seizure. In fact, a number of successful athletes have epilepsy, including retired professional hockey player Gary Howatt. Several years ago, the American Medical Association's Committee on Medical Aspects of Sports published the following statement: 'There is ample evidence that patients with epilepsy will not be affected by indulging in any sport, including football, provided the normal safe-

Table 1: Sports and Epilepsy

Permitted Sports (no restrictions)

aerobics	cross-country	high jumping
archery	skiing	hiking
badminton	curling	jogging
ballet	dancing	lacrosse
baseball	dogsledding	orienteering
basketball	discus throwing	shot-putting
bowling	fencing	soccer
broad jumping	field hockey	table tennis
cricket	fishing	volleyball
croquet	gymnastics	weight lifting
	golfing	wrestling

Possible Sports (reasonable precautions)

bicycling	ice skating	skiing
bobsledding	in-line skating	(downhill)
canoeing	kayaking	sledding
diving	mountain climbing	snowmobiling
football	pole vaulting	swimming
horseback riding	rugby	tennis
hockey	sailing	water polo
hunting	skating	

Prohibited Sports

boxing	polo	scuba diving
bungee jumping	rock climbing	skydiving
hang gliding	sailboarding	snorkeling
jousting	surfing	waterskiing

From Leppik IE: *Contemporary Diagnosis and Management of the Patient With Epilepsy*, 5th ed. Newtown, PA, Handbooks in Health Care, 2000, p 194.

guards for sports participation are followed, including adequate head protection.'

If you enjoy sports, it's important to use common sense when choosing the activities in which to participate (Table 1). Activities such as scuba diving or high-altitude mountain climbing, which can upset the body's metabolic balance, and sports that involve the potential for serious head injury or for serious injury from the loss of consciousness, should be avoided. It's also important to consider the location. For example, swimming in a well-lit pool with lifeguards or others who are aware of your epilepsy is acceptable, but swimming alone in a lake or river is not.

Sexuality and Interpersonal Relations

With the exception of barbiturates or benzodiazepines, antiepileptic drugs (AEDs) usually don't have a major effect on sexual desire. However, AEDs may have a minor effect on some hormones, including estrogen and testosterone. In addition, the fear of having a seizure during a sexual encounter can be inhibiting. With proper counseling, most persons with epilepsy can have normal sexual relations.

The psychological issues of low self-esteem and poorly developed interpersonal skills present greater limitations. Unfortunately, many children with epilepsy are socially isolated in school. In addition, parents may be overprotective, and siblings may be unsupportive. On the other hand, many children with epilepsy who have supportive families develop good self-esteem and integrate well into social relationships. It is important for parents of children with epilepsy to be accepting, to set appropriate safety goals, and to provide a loving environment.

Lack of a driver's license may also present a major limitation, particularly when it comes to dating. Despite these issues, many persons with epilepsy over-

Table 2: First Aid for Seizures

Generalized tonic-clonic seizures

The patient may have a warning, cry out, stiffen, fall, and then rhythmically jerk arms and legs. These movements are very strong and cannot be stopped.

At the onset or during the seizure:

- Help the patient into a prone position
- Remove eyeglasses
- Clear area of harmful objects
- Loosen tight clothing around neck
- Do not restrain the patient
- Do not force any object into the patient's mouth

After the seizure:

- Turn the patient to one side to permit mouth to drain
- Continue to observe the patient until fully awake

If the patient is known to have epilepsy, it is not necessary to call for medical help unless:

---

come barriers and develop stable personal relationships, marry, and have families.

Personal Safety

Persons with epilepsy live with the fear that seizures may strike at any moment, leaving them vulnerable to serious injury or death. In truth, very few persons die during a seizure, but that does not diminish the importance of these concerns. If you, or someone you love has epilepsy, it's important to discuss these concerns with your physician

- An injury has occurred
- Seizures do not stop in 2 to 3 minutes
- A second seizure occurs
- The person requests an ambulance

Complex partial seizures

The patient may stare without focusing, not speak, perform aimless movements, smack lips or appear to chew, fidget with clothes. Sometimes this behavior resembles that of a drunk or drugged person.

During the seizure:

- Do not try to stop or restrain patient
- Guide the patient gently away from harmful objects

After the seizure:

- Stay with the patient until fully alert
- Reassure others that this behavior was medically caused

---

and seek help from the Epilepsy Foundation (EFA). He or she can offer advice. It's also important that you teach your family, friends, teachers and/or coworkers what to do in case of a seizure. They need to know that placing objects into the mouth of someone stricken with a seizure is no longer considered an appropriate intervention because it can damage the teeth and oral tissues. It also might trigger the gag reflex, which can lead to vomiting and the possibility of aspiration pneumonia. Table 2 gives the proper instructions for helping a person who is having a seizure.

Table 3: Laws by State Relating to Driving and Epilepsy*

State	Seizure-Free Period	Physician Reporting
Alabama	6 months, with exceptions	No
Alaska	6 months	No
Arizona	3 months, with exceptions	No
Arkansas	1 year	No
California	**3, 6, or 12 months with exceptions**	**Yes**
Colorado	No set seizure-free period	No
Connecticut	No set seizure-free period	No
Delaware	**No set seizure-free period**	**Yes**
District of Columbia	Annually until seizure-free for 5 years	No
Florida	Upon doctor's recommendation	No
Georgia	1 year	No
Hawaii	1 year, with exceptions	No
Idaho	6 months with strong recommendation from doctor	No
Illinois	No set seizure-free period	No

* Modified from Epilepsy Foundation Legal Advocacy Department and reflects data as of May, 2000. Most states do not require physicians to report epilepsy.

©1996 Epilepsy Foundation. All rights reserved. Reprinted with permission. Latest update available online from EFA: www.EFA.org

State	Seizure-Free Period	Physician Reporting
Indiana	No set seizure-free period	No
Iowa	6 months; less if seizures nocturnal	No
Kansas	6 months; less if seizures nocturnal	No
Kentucky	90 days	No
**Louisiana	6 months, with doctor's statement	No
Maine	3 months or longer	No
Maryland	3 months, with exceptions	No
Massachusetts	6 months, less with doctor's statement	No
Michigan	6 months; less at discretion of department	No
Minnesota	6 months, with exceptions	No
**Mississippi	1 year	No
Missouri	6 months, with doctor's recommendation	No

** No appeal of license denial

\+ No periodic medical updates required

(continued on next page)

Table 3: Laws by State Relating to Driving and Epilepsy* *(continued)*

State	Seizure-Free Period	Physician Reporting
+Montana	No set seizure-free period; doctor's recommendation	No
+Nebraska	3 months	No
Nevada	**3 months, with exceptions**	**Yes**
+New Hampshire	1 year; less at discretion of department	No
New Jersey	**1 year; less on recommendation of Neurological Disorder Committee**	**Yes**
New Mexico	1 year; less with recommendation of Medical Advisory Board	No
New York	1 year, with exceptions	No
North Carolina	6 to 12 months, with exceptions	No
North Dakota	6 months; restricted licenses available after 3 months	No
Ohio	No set seizure-free period	No
Oklahoma	1 year, with exceptions	No
Oregon	**6 months, with exceptions**	**Yes**

Mental Function

Although all major AEDs have some effect on mental functioning, they are generally mild and usually don't worsen with prolonged use. Some commonly de-

State	Seizure-Free Period	Physician Reporting
Pennsylvania	**6 months, with exceptions**	**Yes**
Puerto Rico	No set seizure-free period	No
Rhode Island	18 months; less at the discretion of Dept. of Transportation	No
South Carolina	6 months	No
South Dakota	6-12 months; less with doctor's recommendation	No
Tennessee	6 months, with acceptable medical form	No
Texas	6 months with doctor's recommendation	No
Utah	3 months	No
Vermont	No set seizure-free period	No
Virginia	6 months, with exceptions	No
Washington	6 months, with exceptions	No
West Virginia	1 year, with exceptions	No
Wisconsin	3 months, with acceptable medical form	No
Wyoming	3 months	No

scribed effects include difficulties with memory, lack of energy, and slowness in working with numbers. Sometimes these effects can be more troubling than the seizures, especially if the seizures are simple, partial events. If you or a loved one experience these or other troubling side effects from an AED, it's important that you talk with your doctor. He or she will help you decide if the side effects of the AED are potentially more harmful than the seizures that might occur if you discontinue medication.

Driving

The ability to drive is an important quality-of-life issue for adults with epilepsy. It is a factor in their social lives and, more importantly, it can be a critical issue in finding and keeping a job. Every state has laws that restrict driving by persons with certain medical conditions, including epilepsy. These laws are different from state to state. For example, in some states, a person must be seizure-free for 1 year, while other states either don't specify or use a shorter interval. A few states require that doctors report the names of their epilepsy patients to the Department of Motor Vehicles (DMV) or another state agency. However, most states depend on individual drivers to report this information. Table 3 presents a state-by-state listing of laws related to driving and epilepsy. The DMV or your local EFA chapter should be able to provide additional information on the laws in your state.

When applying for or renewing a driver's license, you will probably be required to fill out a questionnaire that includes a question about whether you have epilepsy, seizures, or a seizure disorder. It's important that you give a truthful answer to this question. If you don't, you can be held liable if you have an accident related to a seizure.

Conclusion

Epilepsy has afflicted humans since ancient times—there are references to it in the Bible and in Greek literature—but not much was known about it until the late 19th century. We've come a long way since the days when many people believed that seizures were caused by demonic possession. Thanks to advances in medical technology during the 20th century, scientists have learned a great deal about the diagnosis and treatment of epilepsy. Although there is still much to learn, the outlook for the future is bright. Persons who are diagnosed with epilepsy today have a better chance to live normal, productive lives.

However, to fully benefit from these advances, you need to be informed about your condition so that you can help yourself or your loved one get the best care possible. Because so much is now known about epilepsy and its treatment, not every physician can possibly know all of the things needed to give the best cost-effective care. Over the last decade, a number of neurologists (physicians who treat disorders of the nervous system) have focused their practices on epilepsy. If your seizures are not completely controlled, or if you have side effects from antiepileptic medicines, you may find it useful to obtain a second opinion from an epilepsy specialist. The American Epilepsy Society is a professional organization specializing in the diagnosis and treatment of epilepsy. Its members are usually the physicians most informed about the latest developments. Another organization, the National Association of Epilepsy Centers (NAEC), has set up standards for epilepsy centers. Because membership is voluntary, not all epilepsy centers belong to this organization. However, you can obtain the criteria recommended for being designated an epilepsy center and find out if your center is a member by writing to: NAEC, 5775 Wayzata Boulevard, Minneapolis, MN, 55416, or by faxing to it: 1-952-525-1560.

Glossary

Absence seizures — The most common seizures of childhood, characterized by a brief lapse of consciousness, eye blinking, staring, and other minor facial movements. Also called *petit mal seizures* in the past.

Atonic seizures – seizures characterized by a sudden loss of muscle tone in the back and legs that causes the person to suddenly drop to the floor.

Aura – an early warning sign of an impending seizure, such as a smell, a sight, a sound, or a sense of uneasiness.

Automatism – automatic bahavior; without conscious effort or thought.

Catamenial epilepsy – seizures that occur only, or primarily, around the days of a woman's menstrual period.

Centrotemporal – refers to the central and temporal regions in the brain.

Clonic seizures – seizures that involve alternate contraction and relaxation of the muscles in rapid succession. They are most common in children.

Corpus callosotomy – a surgical procedure for epilepsy that involves interrupting the spread of seizures from one section of the brain to another by cutting the corpus callosum, a white matter structure connecting both halves of the brain.

Electroencephalogram – a tracing of electrical activity in the brain; EEG.

Epilepsy – a condition in which an individual is susceptible to recurrent seizures because of a brain disorder.

Epileptic focus – the area of the brain involved in localization-related (partial) seizures.

Febrile convulsions – seizures caused by the presence of a high fever in children.

Generalized seizure – a seizure that affects the whole brain.

Grand mal seizures – a term used to describe tonic-clonic seizures.

Hemispherectomy – a surgical treatment for epilepsy that involves removing most or all of one side of the brain.

Ictal activity – refers to brain-wave activity during a seizure.

Idiopathic – having no apparent cause, now considered to be genetic.

Interictal activity – refers to brain-wave activity in between seizures.

Intractable – refers to a disease or condition that does not respond to treatment; refractory.

Ketosis – a condition that occurs when the body is in a fasting state and is forced to use ketones manufactured from fat for fuel.

Lennox-Gastaut syndrome – a syndrome that features an atypical form of absence seizure that often involves atonic, clonic, or tonic-clonic seizures, and mental retardation. There may also be other neurological abnormalities and multiple seizure types. Unlike typical absence epilepsy, it often persists into adulthood.

Lobectomy – a surgical treatment for epilepsy that involves removing some or all of the section of a lobe of the brain where the seizures originate.

Localization-related seizure – a seizure in which the abnormal activity is confined to only one part of the brain; partial seizure.

Mesial temporal lobe sclerosis — Seizure syndrome originating with a febrile seizure in childhood. Involves only one temporal lobe and may be corrected surgically.

Multiple subpial transection – a surgical procedure for epilepsy that involves interfering with the spread of seizures by making a small incision in the brain.

Myoclonic seizures – seizures that involve quick muscle jerks in one or several areas of the body.

Occipital – a lobe in the back part of the brain, which controls vision.

Paroxysms – sudden unexpected events; when referring to seizures, a sudden and intense electrical discharge in the brain.

Partial seizure – a localization-related seizure.

Petit mal – a term used to describe absence seizures.

Physiologic – related to the function of the body.

Postictal – referring to the period immediately following a seizure.

Prodromal – referring to symptoms that give early warning of an attack.

Psychogenic – related to the mental process involving emotional issues.

Pyknolepsy – childhood absence seizures; based on the Greek word *pyknos*, which means thick or frequent.

Refractory – resistant to treatment; intractable.

Rolandic epilepsy – a benign childhood epilepsy that usually begins between the ages of 3 and 13. Most children outgrow it by age 13.

Seizure – an abnormal electrical discharge in the brain that can result in sudden involuntary change in any activity coordinated by the brain, including mental confusion, loss of consciousness, violent, uncontrollable movements of the arms and legs, or other phenomena.

Symptomatic cryptogenic – epilepsy of undetermined (cryptogenic) origin, but suspected of being a symptom of brain injury.

Symptomatic localization-related epilepsies – epilepsies with specific, identifiable causes.

Syncope – a brief loss of consciousness caused by loss of oxygen to the brain; fainting spell.

Syndrome – a group of symptoms that collectively characterize an abnormal condition or disorder.

Teratogenicity – refers to a drug's potential for causing birth defects.

Tonic seizures – seizures that involve continuous tightening of the muscles in the face and body, with bending of the upper part of the body and extension of the legs.

Tonic-clonic seizures – the most dramatic of all seizures. They begin with tightening of the muscles and progress to alternating contraction and relaxation of the muscles, which causes the arms and legs to jerk violently; also referred to as grand mal seizures.

West's syndrome – infantile spasms characterized by bending at the neck, waist, arms, and legs, with the arms either drawn away from or toward the body.

Index

A

Abbott Laboratories 50, 63

abdominal pain 44, 50, 51

abnormal brain activity 32

abnormal involuntary movements 44

abscess 20

acetazolamide (AK-Zol®, Diamox®) 57

acidosis 82

Adams-Stokes syndrome 28

aerobics 100

aggressiveness 50

AK-Zol® 57

alcohol 29, 47, 94

allopurinol 47

Alzheimer's disease 20, 67

American Academy of Pediatrics 51

American Epilepsy Society 85, 109

American Medical Association's Committee on Medical Aspects of Sports 99

Americans with Disabilities Act (ADA) 99

amiodarone 47

analgesics 48

anemia 61

aneurysms 20

anorexia 44, 50, 65

antiarrhythmic agents 47

anticoagulants 44, 47

antiepileptic drugs (AEDs) 35-37, 39-42, 52, 54, 57-60, 62, 64, 66, 67, 69, 75-78, 81, 82, 87-94, 106, 108, 109

antineoplastic agents 47

aplastic anemia 61

archery 100

arteriovenous malformation (AVM) 20

aspiration pneumonia 103

ataxia 43, 52, 60, 63, 65

atrioventricular block 28

auras 81, 110

automatism 110

B

badminton 100

ballet 100

barbiturates (phenobarbital) 55, 56, 89, 101

baseball 100

basketball 100

Bellatal® 38

benzodiazepines 38, 94, 101

bicycling 100

birth control 89

birth defects 89, 91, 92, 93, 114

birth trauma 6

bleomycin 47

blood dyscrasias 20

blurred vision 44

bobsledding 100

bowling 100

boxing 100

brain injury 114

brain surgery 79

brain tumor 35, 67

breast-feeding 90, 94

broad jumping 100

bromide 37-39

bungee jumping 100

C

caffeine 30, 94

calcium 82

cancer 30

canoeing 100

carbamazepine (Carbatrol®, Tegretol®, Tegretol®XR) 34, 38, 42-45, 47, 48, 56, 58, 61-65, 67, 69, 70, 89, 92

Carbatrol® 34, 38, 89

cardiac arrhythmias 28

CAT scan 17

central nervous system (CNS) 5, 8, 18, 25, 36, 50, 52, 54, 65

cerebrovascular ischemia 28

Cerebyx® 34, 38, 46, 47

Charlie Foundation 83

cherry-red spot myoclonus 23

chloramphenicol 47, 56

chlorpheniramine 47

cimetidine 44, 47

cisplatin 47

Citizens United for Research in Epilepsy 85

cleft lip and palate 92

clonazepam (Klonopin®) 38, 44, 48, 52
clonic activity 27
complex partial seizure 12
compliance 45, 83, 91
computed tomography (CT) 33
confusion 44, 65
constipation 44, 50, 82
contraception 89
convulsions 15, 21, 26, 75
corpus callosotomy 73, 74, 110
corpus callosum 74
corticosteroids 45, 48, 56
cricket 100
croquet 100
cross-country skiing 100
curling 100
cyclosporine 48, 56
cysticercosis 20

D

danazol 44
dancing 100
decreased alertness 59
decreased appetite 62
dementia 56
Depacon™ 38, 49, 89, 92
Depakene® 38, 48, 49, 89, 92
Depakote® 38, 48, 49, 50
Depakote® Sprinkle 49, 50
Department of Motor Vehicles (DMV) 108
Depo-Provera® 89
depression 38, 44, 56
desipramine (Norpramin®) 56
diabetes 71, 86
Diamox® 57
diarrhea 44, 50, 59
Diastat® 34, 53
diazepam (Diastat®, Valium®) 34, 44
dicumarol 47
differential diagnosis 27
difficulty with concentration 63
digitoxin 47, 56
digoxin 66
Dilantin® 38, 45, 46, 67, 89
diltiazem 44
discus throwing 100
disopyramide 47
disulfiram (Antabuse®) 47

divalproex sodium (Depakote®) 48-50, 92

diving 100

dizziness 40, 43, 59, 62, 63, 65, 66

dogsledding 100

Donnatal® 38

dopamine 48

double vision 43, 60, 65

doxorubicin 56

doxycycline 44, 47, 56

driving 36, 98, 101, 104, 106, 108

drop attacks 74, 75

drowsiness 40, 43, 50, 52, 54, 55, 60

dry mouth 40, 44, 59

dysphasia 44

dysplasia 20

dyssynergia cerebellaris myoclonica 23

E

early infantile epileptic encephalopathy 22

early myoclonic encephalopathy 22

easy bruising 44, 51

edema 51

Elan 53

electrodes 31, 33, 86

electroencephalogram (EEG) 17, 18, 24, 31-33, 36, 63, 69, 70, 73, 76, 77, 111

electrolyte imbalance 29

emotional stress 91

employment 76, 97, 98

encephalitis 20

Epilepsy 5, 6, 8, 9, 11, 13, 16, 25-27, 30, 35, 36, 38, 39, 53, 59, 60, 62, 66, 67, 70, 72, 73, 75-77, 79, 81, 83-90, 93, 95, 97, 98, 99, 101, 102, 104, 106, 108-112, 114

absence 16, 22, 23

akinetic 54

benign 35

benign childhood 22, 113

benign childhood with centrotemporal spikes 19

benign myoclonic 48

benign neonatal familial convulsions 21

benign partial 22, 23

benign psychomotor 22

benign rolandic 19, 69

catamenial 88, 110

Epilepsy *(continued)*
- childhood absence 21, 24
- childhood epilepsy with occipital spikes 19
- epilepsy with generalized convulsive seizures 22
- epilepsy with grand mal on awakening 23
- epilepsy with myoclonic absences 22
- epilepsy with photosensitivity 23
- generalized 18, 21, 48
- idiopathic 18, 21, 24, 48
- incidence of 5
- intractable 72, 82
- juvenile absence 23
- juvenile myoclonic (JME) 21, 23, 24, 52, 70
- localization-related 18
- mesial temporal lobe sclerosis (MTS) 19
- mild 6
- myoclonic 22, 23, 25, 48
- myoclonic in infancy 22
- nonspecific etiology 21
- partial 57
- photosensitive 52
- progressive myoclonic 48
- secondary 18
- special syndromes 18
- specific syndromes 21
- stimulus-sensitive 48
- symptomatic 21, 24
- symptomatic cryptogenic 20
- symptomatic localization-related 19, 114
- typical absence 112
- uncontrollable 7
- undetermined for focal or generalized 18

Epilepsy Foundation (EFA) 5, 73-75, 77, 85, 87, 88, 103, 104, 108

Equal Employment Opportunity Commission (EEOC) 99

erythromycin 44, 67

estrogen 101

ethosuximide (Zarontin®) 38, 44, 47, 48, 54, 89

exercise 94

eyelid myoclonia absences 23

F

family history 30

fatigue 31, 44, 62, 65, 91

febrile convulsions 22, 30, 111

felbamate (Felbatol®) 34, 38, 58, 61, 62

Felbatol® 34, 58, 61, 62

fencing 100

fever 8, 9, 26, 44

field hockey 100

fifth-day fits 22

folic acid 47, 94

Food and Drug Administration (FDA) 59, 61, 79, 81, 82, 85

football 99, 100

fosphenytoin (Cerebyx®) 34, 38, 45-47

G

gabapentin (Neurontin®) 34, 38, 57-60, 70, 71, 89

Gabitril® 34, 38, 58, 63

gastric distress 44

gastrointestinal (GI) disturbances 38, 50, 54

Gene Discovery Project 85

genetic syndromes 6

gingival hyperplasia 47

Glaxo Wellcome 60

glioma 20

glossitis 44

golfing 100

grand mal seizures 13, 111, 114

griseofulvin 56

gymnastics 100

H

haloperidol (Haldol®) 44, 56

hamartomas 20

hand tremor 50

hang gliding 100

harelip 92

head injury 20, 30, 67, 69, 101

head trauma 8, 9, 36

headache 44, 60

heart defects 92

heart disease 30, 86

heartburn 50

hemispherectomy 73, 74, 111

hemorrhage 20

hepatic enzymes 65

hepatic metabolism 64

hepatitis 61
herbal products 30
herpes zoster 71
heterotopias 20
high blood pressure 70
high cholesterol levels 82
high jumping 100
hiking 100
hockey 100
horseback riding 100
hunting 100
hyperactivity 50
hyperglycinemia 48
hyperkinesia 56
hyperplasia 47
hyperventilate 32
hyperventilation 28
hyperventilation-induced syncope 28
hypoglycemia 29
hyponatremia 64
hypotension 28, 54, 59
hypovolemia 28
hypoxia 29

I

ice skating 100
ictal activity 111
in-line skating 100
infantile epileptic encephalopathy 22
infantile hemiplegia 20
infantile spasms 22, 24, 48, 114
insomnia 62
interictal activity 111
International Classification of Epileptic Seizures 14, 18
International League Against Epilepsy (ILAE) 11, 17
intrauterine device (IUD) 89
irritability 93
isoniazid 44, 47

J

jaundice 51
jogging 100
Johns Hopkins University 81
jousting 100
juvenile Gaucher's 23
juvenile neuronal ceroid lipofuscinosis (NCL) 23

K

kayaking 100
Keppra™ 34, 38, 58, 66, 89
ketogenic diet 6, 81, 82
ketosis 112
kidney stones 63, 65, 82
Klonopin® 38, 52
Kojewnikoff's syndrome 23

L

labor and delivery 90, 93, 95
lack of energy 66, 107
lacrosse 100
Lafora's body disease 23
Lamictal® 34, 58, 60, 89
lamotrigine (Lamictal®) 34, 38, 58, 60, 61, 66, 70, 89
Landau-Kleffner syndrome 23
Lennox-Gastaut syndrome 16, 22, 24, 25, 48, 61, 112
lethargy 51, 64
level of independence 76
levetiracetam (Keppra™) 34, 38, 58, 66, 89
lightheadedness 43
lithium 45
lobectomy 70, 73, 74, 112
localization-related seizure 113
Lorezapam® 38
loss of appetite 51
loss of seizure control 51

M

magnetic resonance imaging (MRI) 17, 33, 70, 73, 76
malformation 20
massive jerking movements 74
Mayo Clinic 81
mebendazole 44
memory 73, 107
meningitis 20
menopause 87
menstrual cycle 87-89
mental function 98, 106
mental retardation 112
mental slowing 56
meperidine 48
mesial temporal sclerosis 19, 73, 75, 112
metastatic tumors 20

methadone 48
metoprolol 56
mexiletine 47
micturition syncope 28
mild fatigue 59
mild nausea 40
mitochondrial encephalopathy 23
motor ability 73
mountain climbing 100, 101
multiple sclerosis 20
multiple subpial transection (MST) 73, 112
muscle weakness 59
myoclonic encephalopathy 22
myoclonic movements 70
myoclonic syndromes 65
myoclonus 48
Mysoline® 38, 56, 57, 94

N

narkosenide 35
National Association of Epilepsy Centers (NAEC) 85, 109
National Institutes of Health 84
nausea 11, 40, 43, 50, 51, 54, 59, 62
Neurontin® 34, 38, 57, 58, 60, 89
nicotinamide 44
noncompliance 37
Norplant® 89
nortriptyline (Pamelor®) 56
nystagmus 44, 59

O

occipital spikes 19
oculomotor disturbances 44
oral contraceptives 47, 66
orienteering 100
Ortho-McNeil Pharmaceutical 62
over-the-counter drugs (OCDs) 30, 40, 41, 67
oxcarbazepine (Trileptal®) 34, 38, 58, 64, 89

P

pancreatitis 50
paresthesias 44, 63
Parke-Davis 54
paroxysmal tachycardia 28
paroxysms 113

partial loss of vision 73
perinatal injuries 20
peripheral neuritis 44
personal safety 98
personality changes 52
petechial hemorrhage 44
petit mal 13, 113
phenobarbital 26, 38, 39, 42, 44, 45, 51, 52, 55, 64, 69, 93, 94
phenothiazines 56
phenytoin (Dilantin®) 38, 42, 44-48, 52, 53, 56, 58, 61-70, 89
photosensitive myoclonus 48
pole-vaulting 100
polo 100
poor responsiveness 64
poor sucking 93
positron emission tomography (PET) 17, 76
postictal period 29, 113
postpartum 95
pregabin 34
pregnancy 86, 87, 89, 90, 92-94
primidone (Mysoline®) 38, 42, 44, 45, 47, 56, 94

prodromal 113
prodromal symptoms 28
Progestasert® 89
progressive myoclonus epilepsies 23
propoxyphene hydrochloride 44
propranolol 56
psychogenic 113
psychomotor slowing 63
puberty 87
pyknolepsy 21, 22, 113

Q

Quadrinal® 38
quality-of-life 97, 108
quinidine 47, 56

R

Ramsay Hunt syndrome 23
rapid breathing 93
rash 59
Rasmussen's syndrome 20
reflex cardiac arrhythmia 28
refractory 37, 113
Rehabilitation Act of 1973 99

relationships with family and friends 76

rifampin 47

Roche 52, 53

rock climbing 100

rubella 20

rufinamide 35

rugby 100

S

safety 102

sailboarding 100

sailing 100

sclerosis 20

scuba diving 100, 101

sedation 29, 38, 50, 56

Seizure 9, 15, 27, 28, 35-37, 40-42, 57, 61, 63, 64, 67, 68, 70-74, 76, 78, 81, 84, 86-93, 95, 97-99, 101-107, 109, 110, 112-114

   absence (petit mal) 13, 14, 15, 24, 42, 45, 48, 51, 57, 110, 112, 113

   akinetic 48

   atonic 13, 14, 16, 25, 42, 45, 48, 52, 61, 110, 112

   atypical absence 13, 15, 25, 48

   axial tonic 25

   clonic 13-16, 110, 112

   complex 56

   complex partial 11-14, 19, 42, 45, 54, 60, 70, 71, 73, 91, 103

   epileptic focus 11

   febrile 26, 51, 53, 112

   generalized 9, 11-14, 19, 21, 42, 60, 61, 70, 81, 111

   generalized tonic-clonic (grand mal) 24, 42, 45, 48, 52, 54-57, 69, 74, 75, 91, 95, 102

   ictal phase 18

   interictal phase 18

   localization-related 112

   myoclonic 13-15, 22-24, 42, 45, 48, 52, 54, 112

   neonatal 55

   nonepileptic 27, 28, 35

   partial 11, 12, 14, 19, 42, 48, 56, 57, 59-61, 63-65, 75, 81, 112

   partial (localization-related) 111, 113

   partial epileptic 9

   partial onset 62, 66

   provoked 29

Seizure *(continued)*
- psychogenic 9
- pyknolepsy (childhood absence) 113
- recurrent 5, 8, 35, 45, 76, 111
- second 36, 68, 69, 103
- secondarily generalized 11, 12, 14, 19, 48, 59, 60
- simple 42, 73
- simple partial 11, 12, 45, 55, 56, 107
- single 8, 27, 36, 67
- situation-related 26
- tonic 13-16, 48, 114
- tonic-clonic (grand mal) 13, 14, 16, 19, 25, 30, 48, 70, 111, 112, 114
- typical absence (petit mal) 13, 15, 21, 48
- unclassified epileptic 13
- unprovoked 29
- withdrawal 69

self-esteem 36, 101
self-image 76
severe myoclonic epilepsy in infants 22
sexuality and interpersonal relations 98
sharp waves 31
shot-putting 100
sickle cell anemia 20
sinoatrial block 28
skating 100
skeletal muscle relaxants 48
skiing (downhill) 100
skin eruptions 38
skin rash 60
skydiving 100
sledding 100
sleep 23, 94
sleep deprivation 29, 30
sleep disturbances 59, 93
slurred speech 59
smoking 94
snorkeling 100
snowmobiling 100
soccer 100
somnolence 63, 65, 66
sore throat 44
speech disorders 63, 73
spikes 22, 23, 31, 70
spikes and waves 22, 23, 36, 63
spina bifida 92
sports 97, 99-101

St. John's Wort 83, 84
status epilepticus (SE) 13, 45
Stevens-Johnson syndrome 61
stimulants 29
stomatitis 44
stroke 20, 30, 36, 67, 68, 70, 73
stunted growth 82
Sturge-Weber syndrome 20
substance abuse 29, 30
sudden involuntary movements 70
sulfonamides 47
surfing 100
surgery 6, 30, 72-77, 81
sweating 11
swelling of the brain 73
swimming 100, 101
symptomatic cryptogenic 114
syncope 27, 28, 114
syndrome 114

T

table tennis 100
tachycardia 28
talkativeness 44
Tegretol® 38, 43, 89, 92
Tegretol® XR 34, 42, 43
temporal lobectomy 70
tennis 100
teratogenicity 93, 114
testosterone 101
theophylline 44, 48, 56
thyroid hormones 45
tiagabine (Gabitril®) 34, 38, 58, 63, 64, 70
tinnitus 44
tiredness 62
tongue biting 30
tonic-clonic status epilepticus 53
Topamax® 34, 38, 58, 62, 63
topiramate (Topamax®) 34, 38, 58, 62
toxoplasmosis 20
tracings 31, 33
travel 30
trazodone (Desyrel®) 47
tremor 59, 93
Trileptal® 34, 38, 58, 64, 65, 89
trimethoprim 47
troleandomycin 44

tuberculosis 47
tumor 20, 67, 68

U

UCB Pharma 66

uncoordinated movements 60

Unverricht-Lundborg disease 23

V

vagus nerve stimulator (VNS) 6, 79, 80, 81, 86

Valium® 38, 53, 94

valproate (Depakote®, Depacon™) 34, 38, 44, 47-52, 58, 60, 62, 70, 89, 92

valproate therapy 51

valproic acid (Depakene®) 48, 49, 61

vasovagal attack 28

venous sclerosis 46

venous thrombosis 20

verapamil 44, 56

vinblastine 47

vitamin B 82

vitamin C 82

vitamin K 93

volleyball 100

vomiting 43, 50, 51, 54, 93, 103

W

Wallace Laboratories 61

warfarin 66

water polo 100

waterskiing 100

weight lifting 100

weight loss 62

West's syndrome 22, 24, 114

Women and Epilepsy Initiative 88

work stress 30

wrestling 100

Z

Zarontin® 38, 54, 89

Zonegran™ 34, 38, 58, 65, 66

zonisamide (Zonegran™) 34, 38, 58, 65